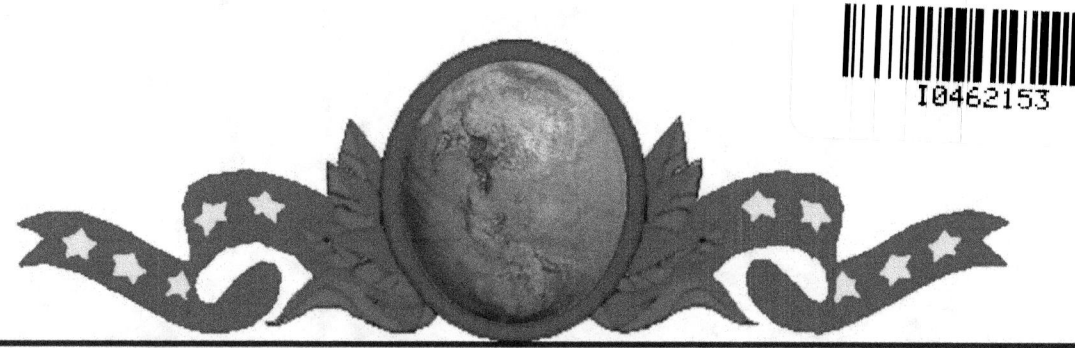

Real World
Colouring Book
For Advanced Users & Adults

Copyright 2019 By John Boom

50 Images

**Created From Real Life Photos
For You To Colour As You Please.**

ISBN 978-0-359-78772-2

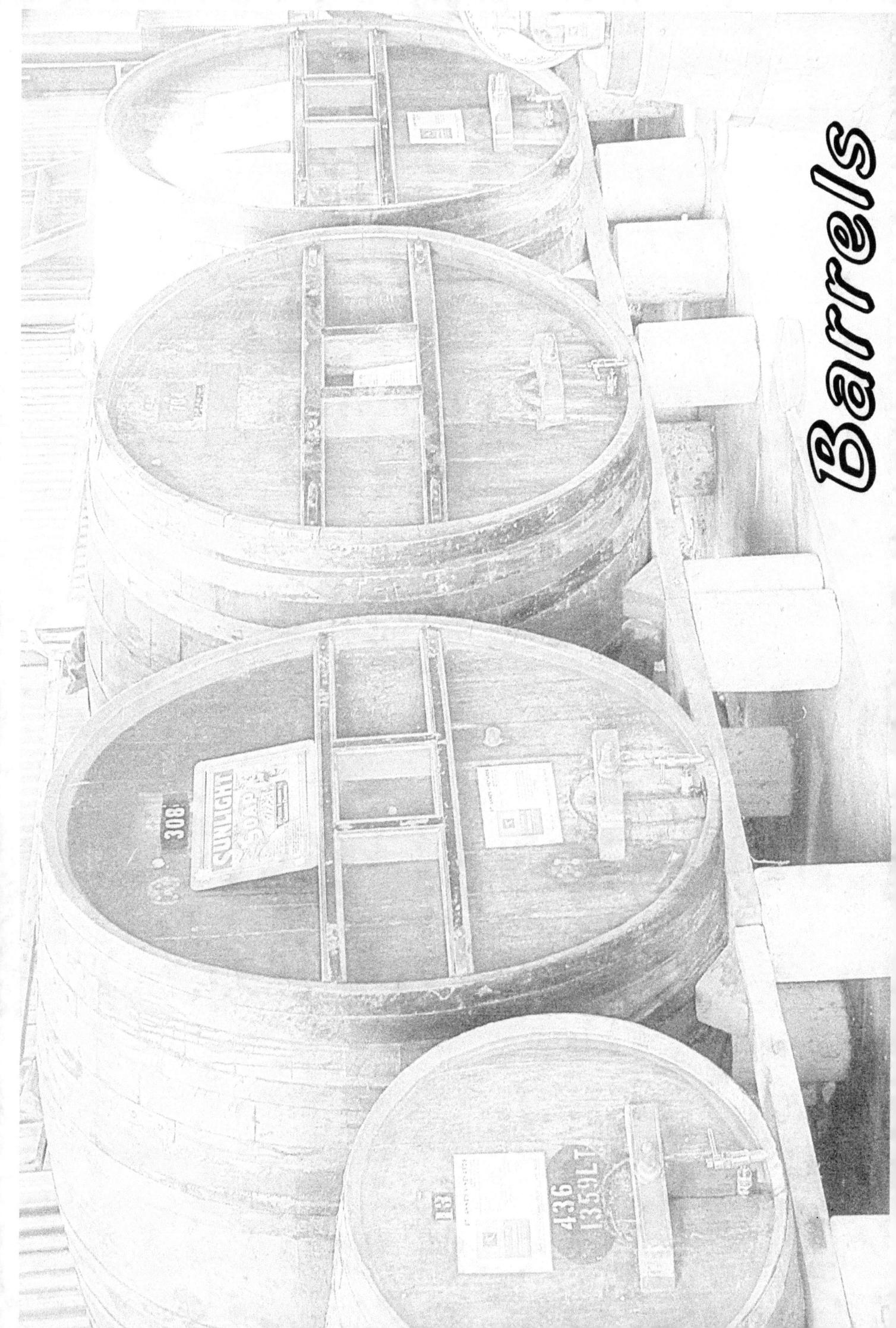

Barrels

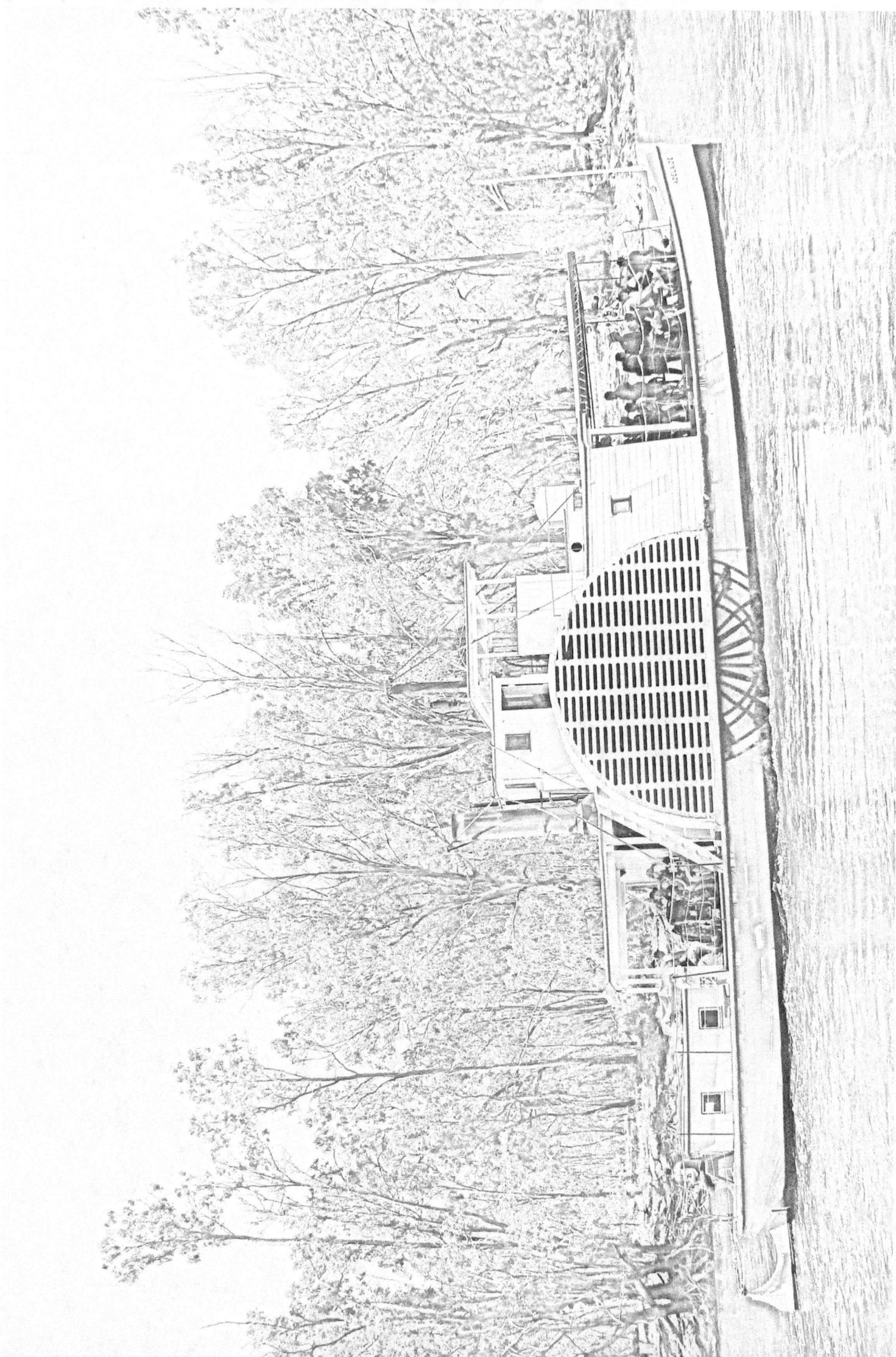

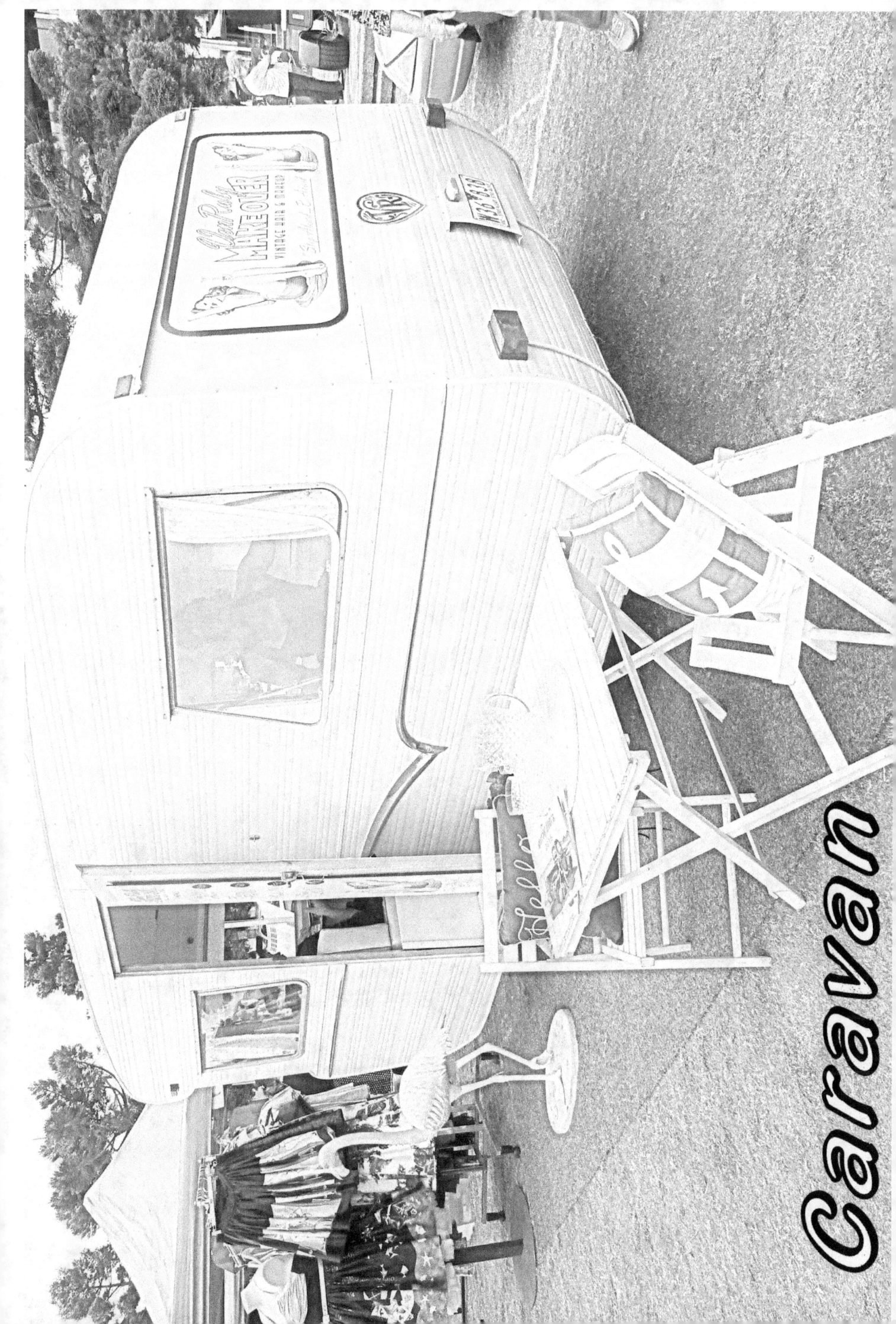

Caravan

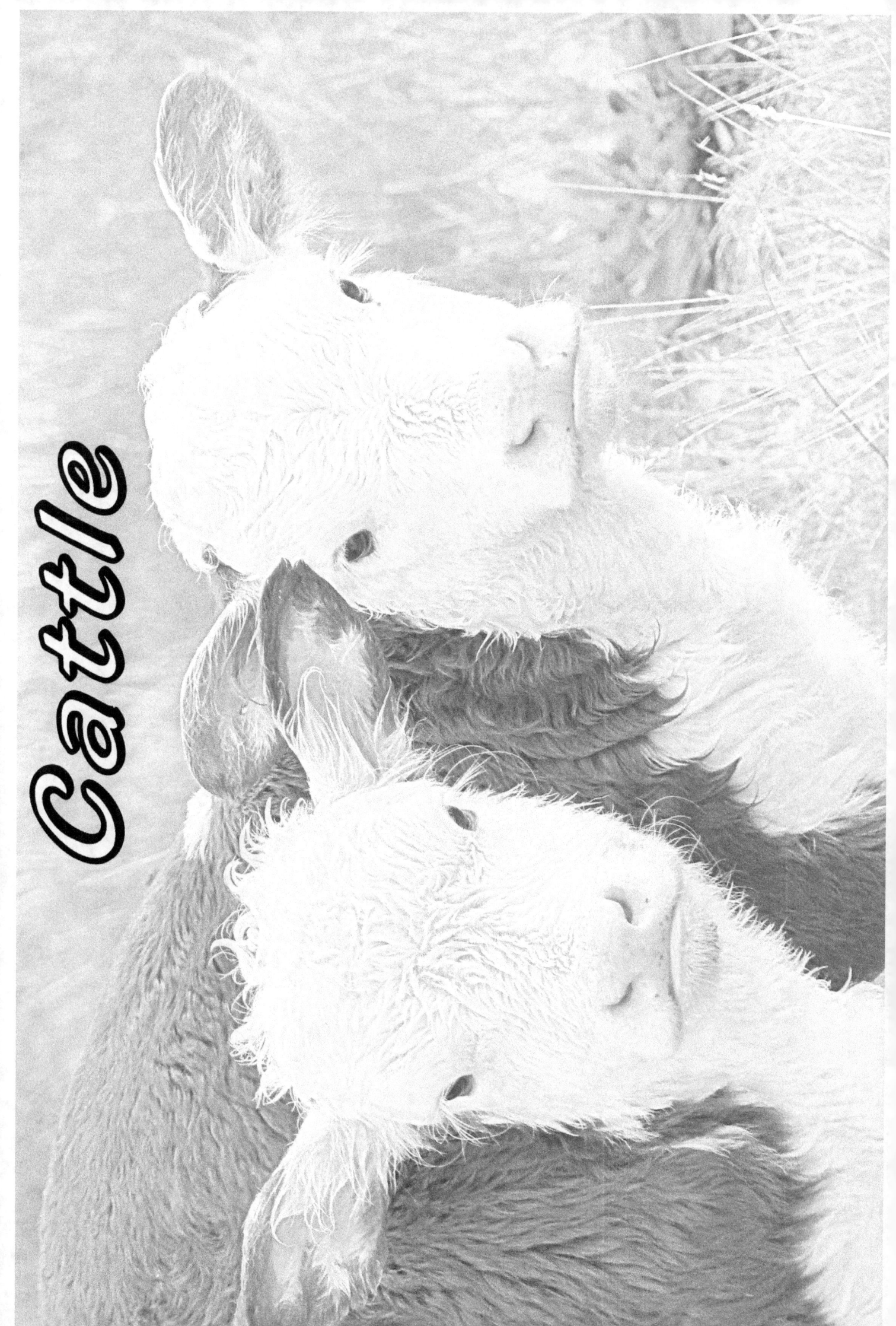

Cattle

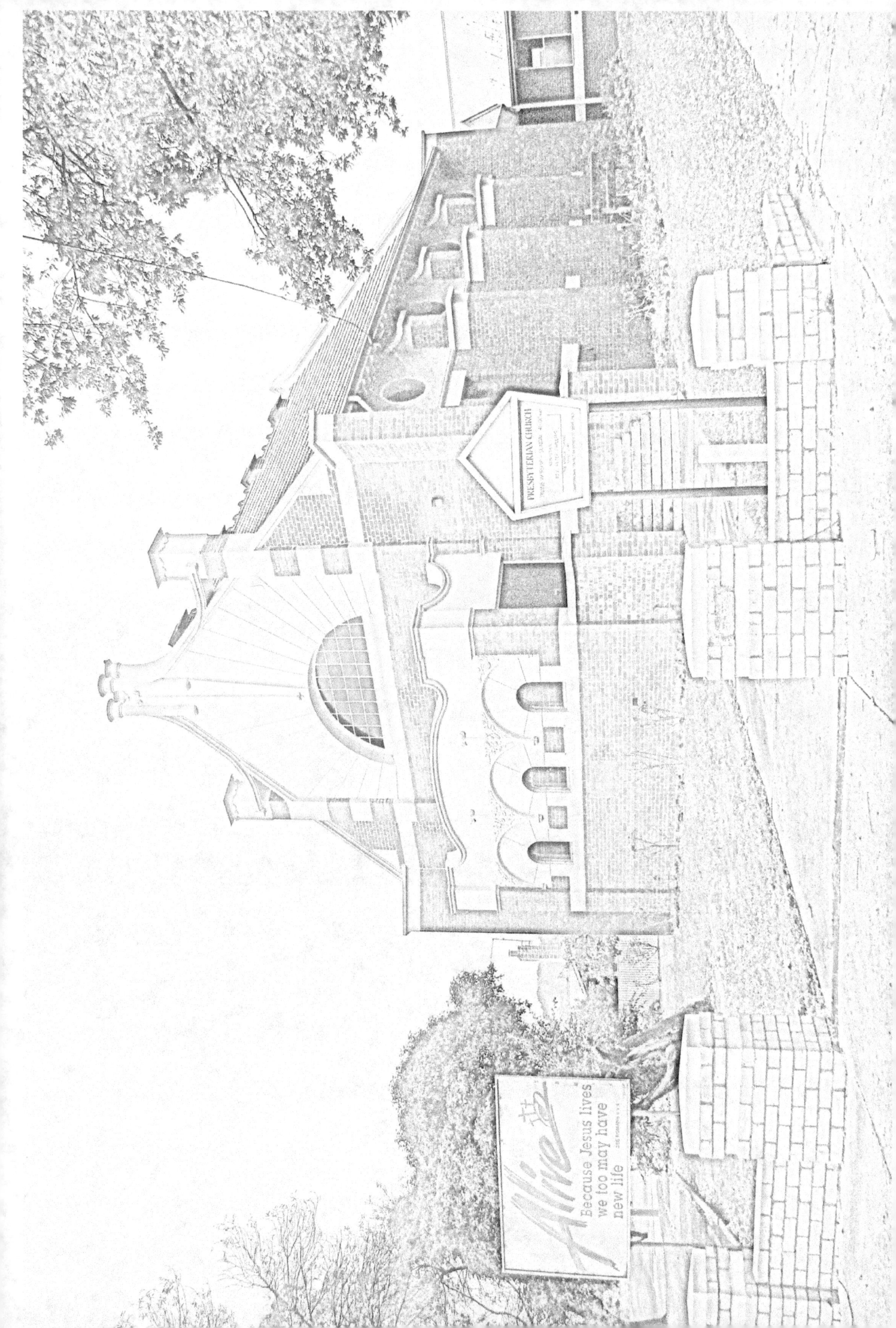

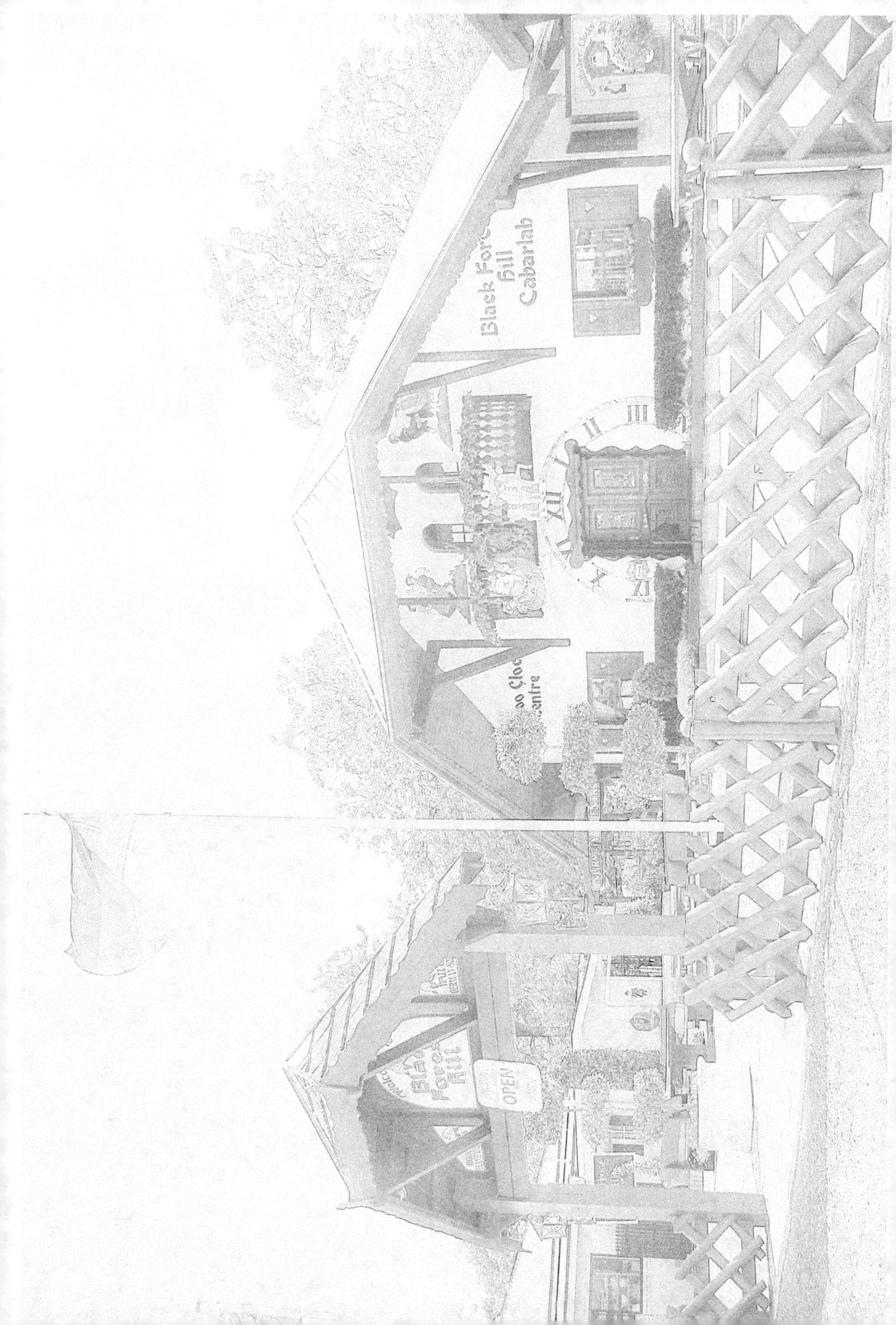

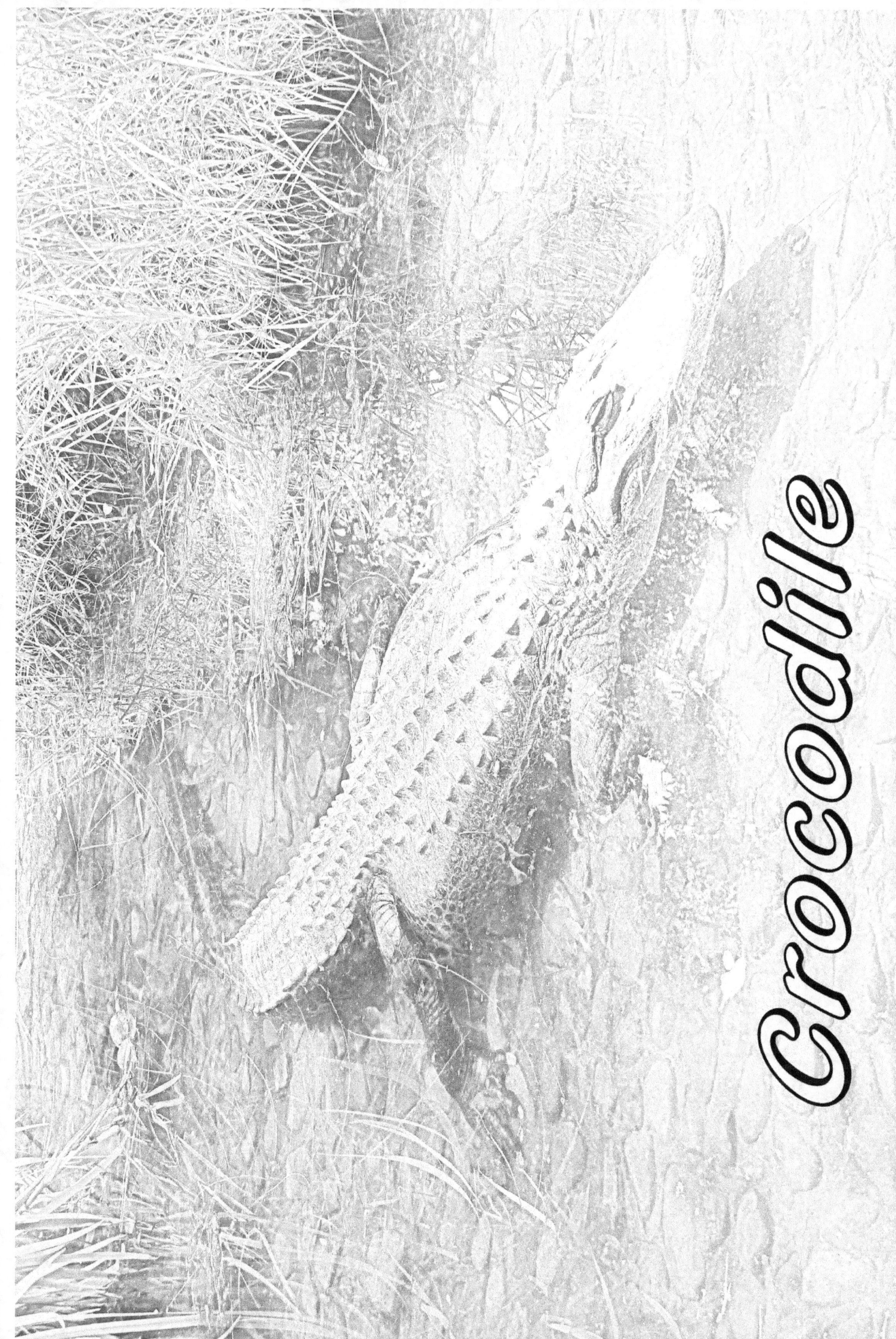

Crocodile

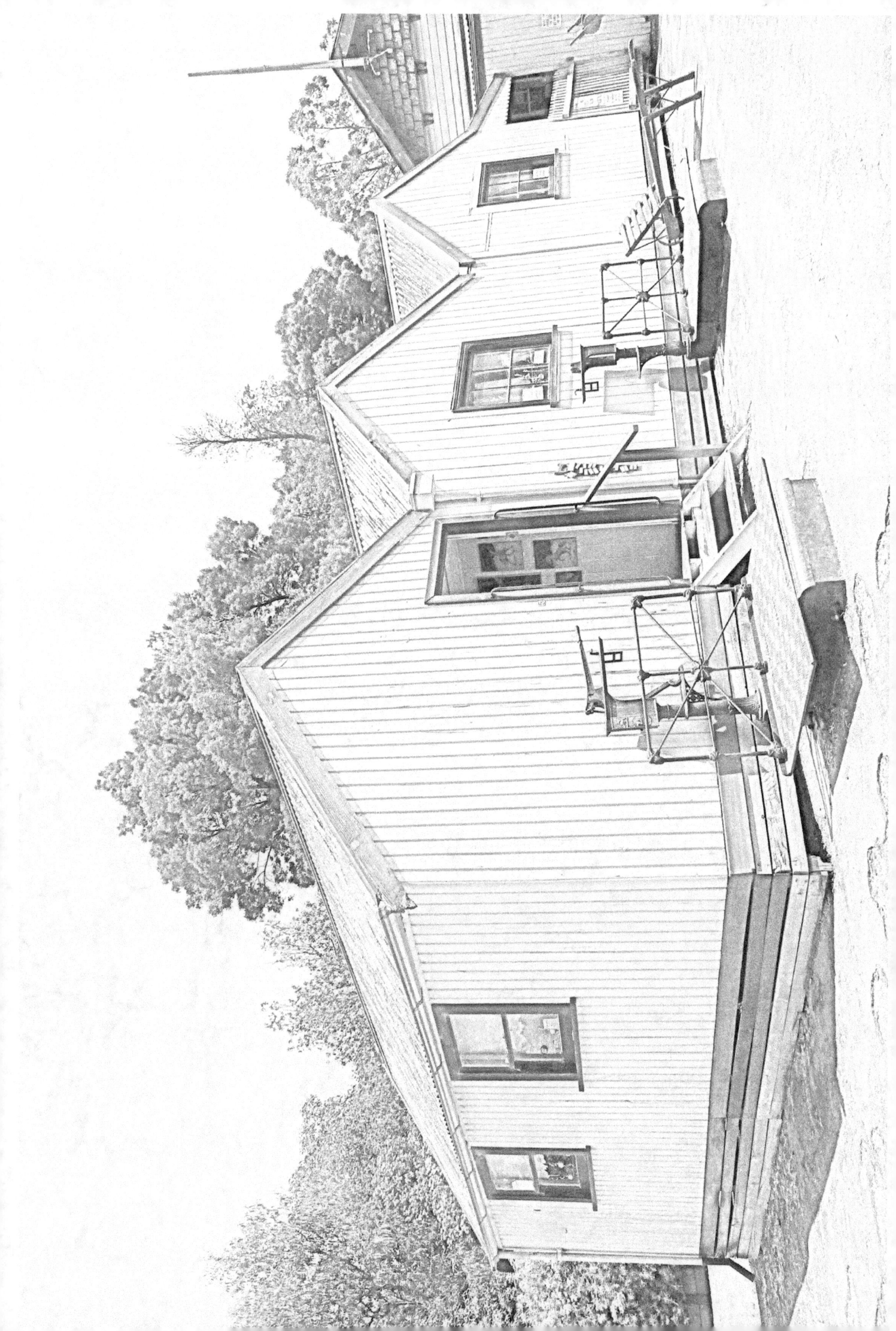

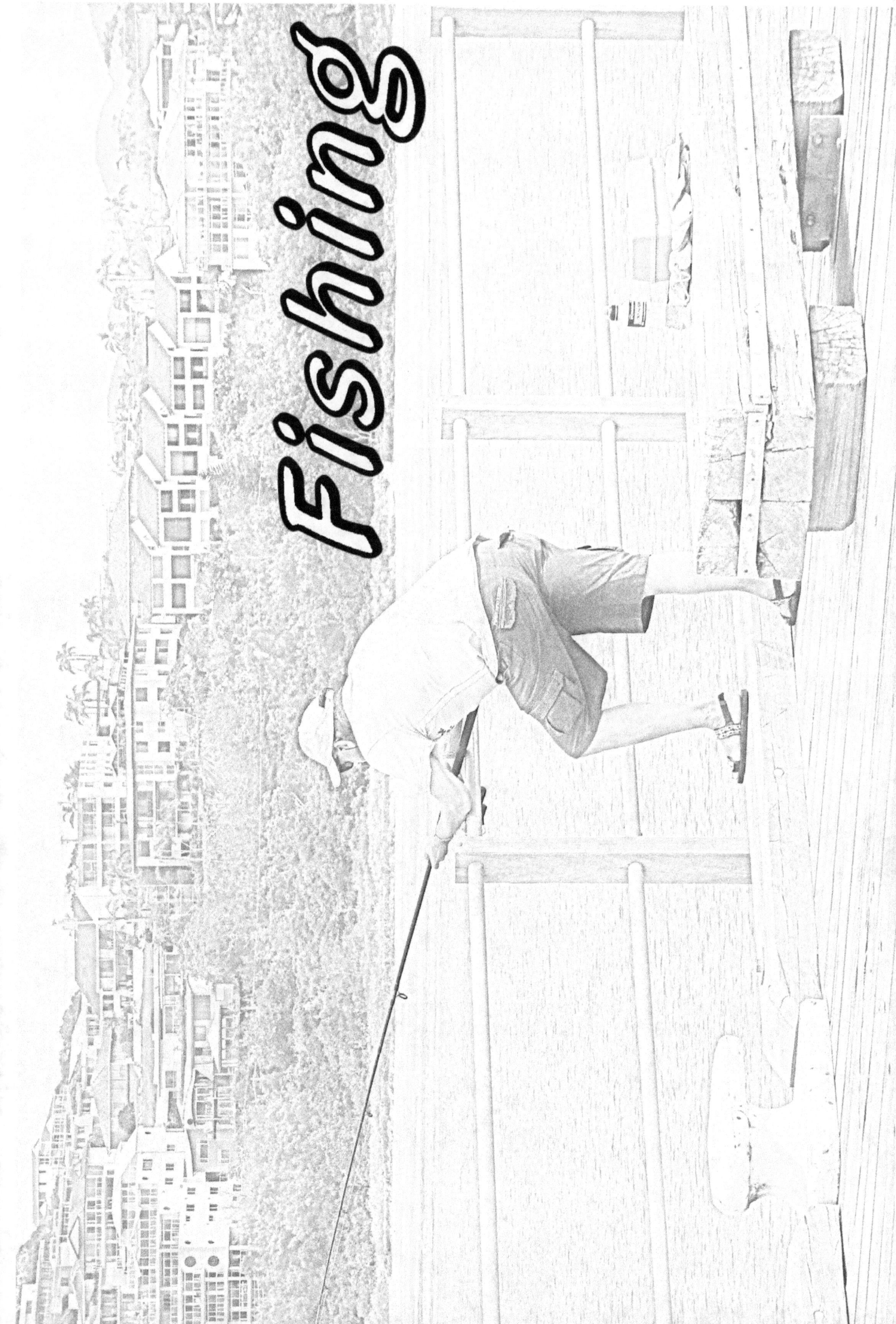

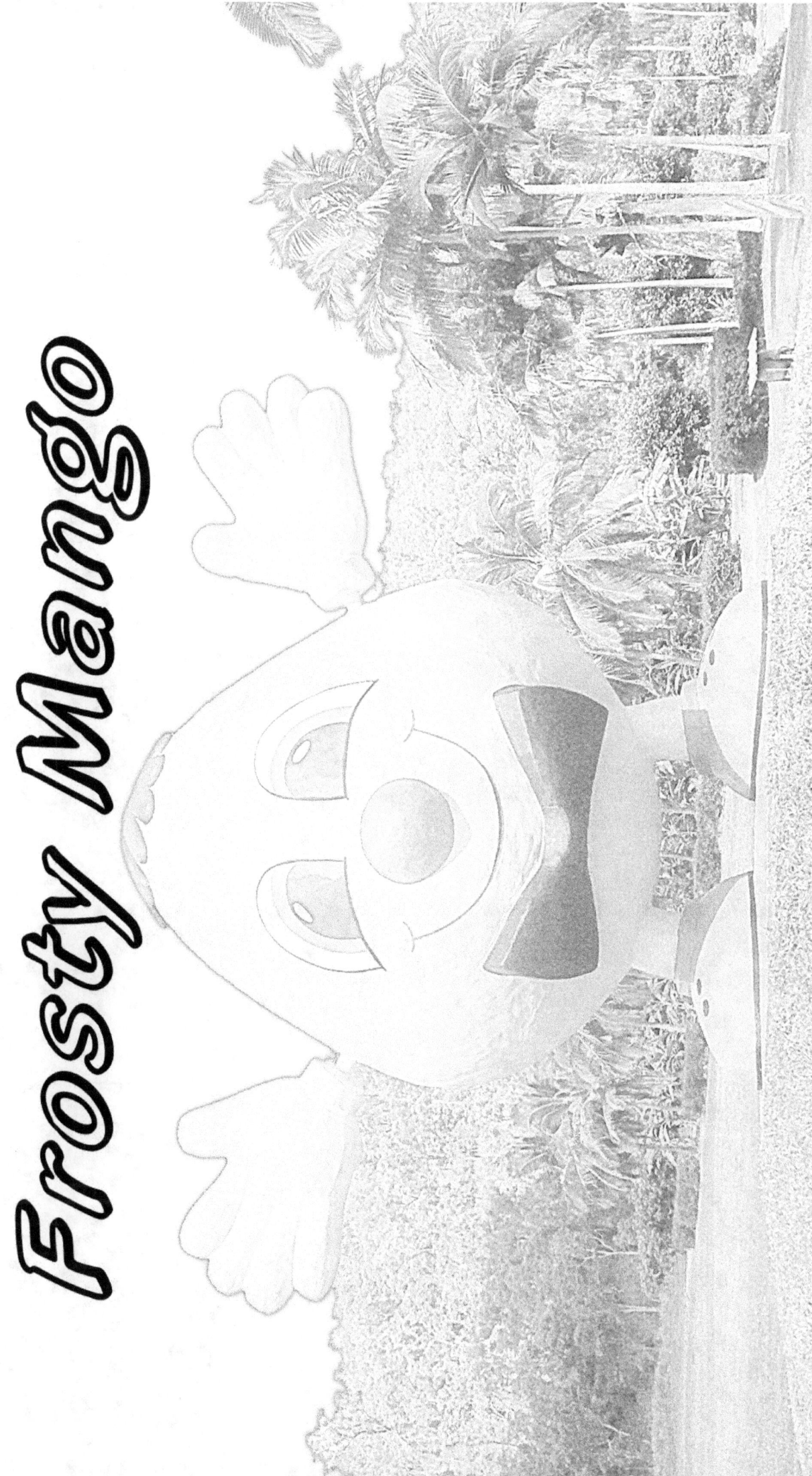

Frosty Mango

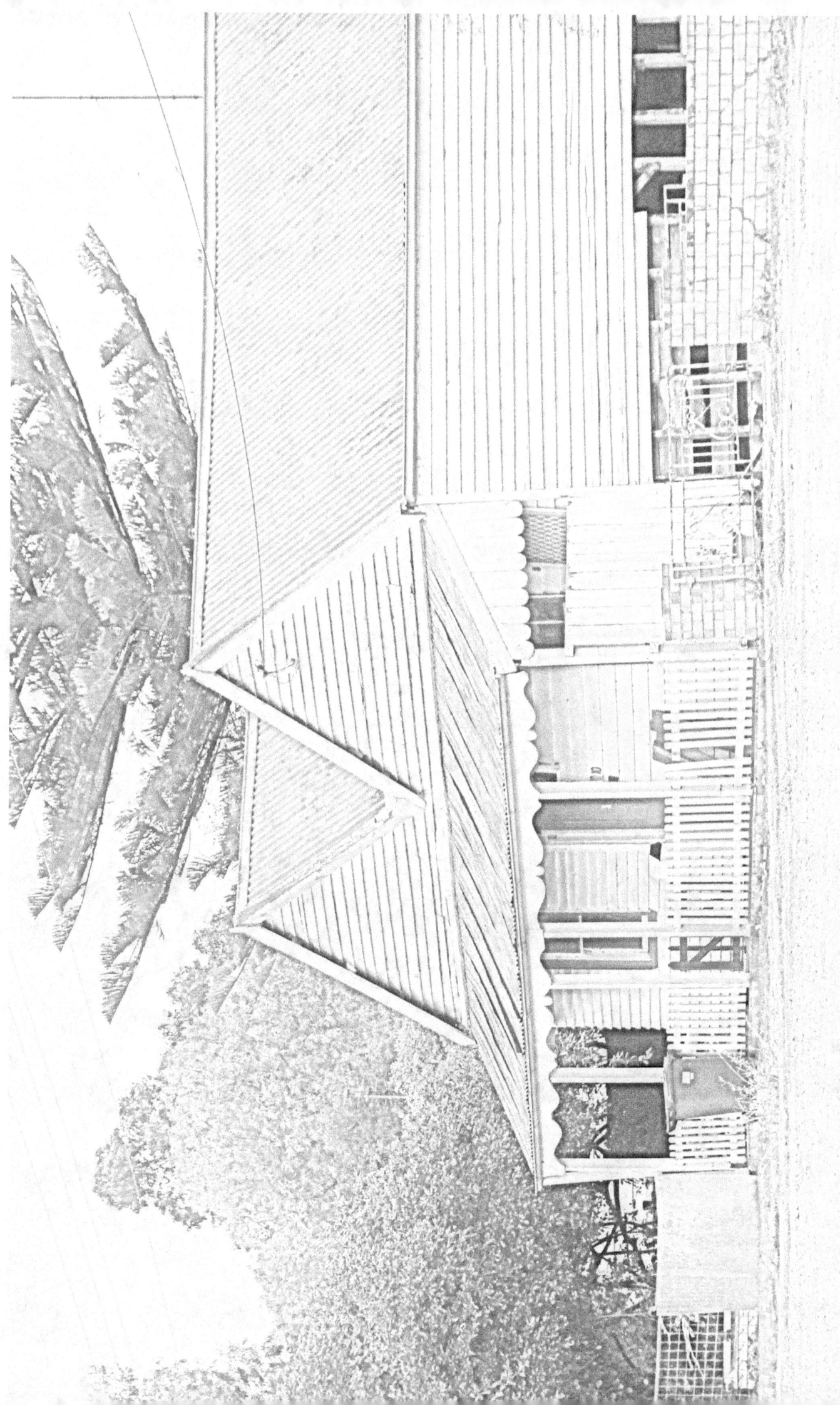

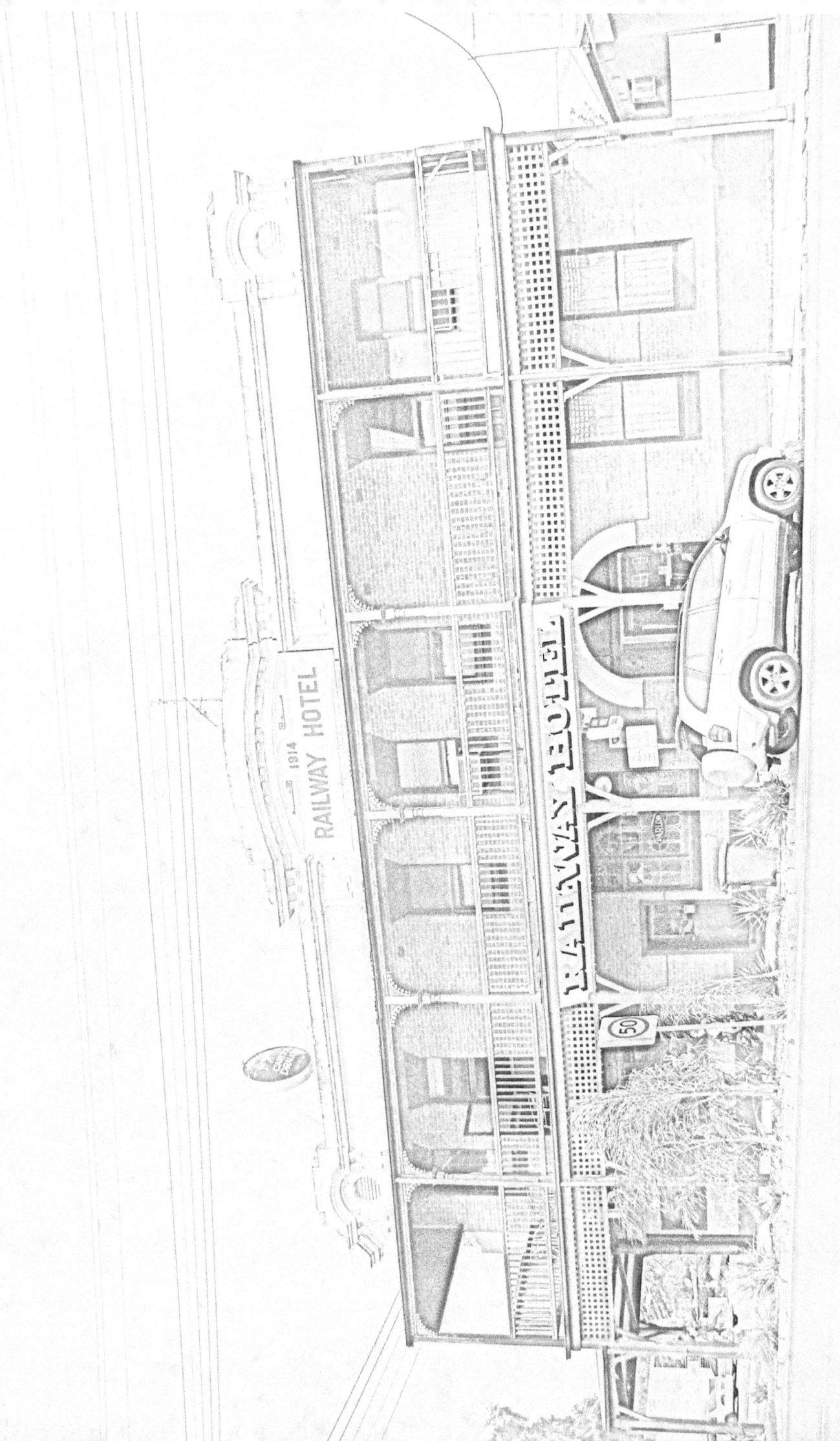

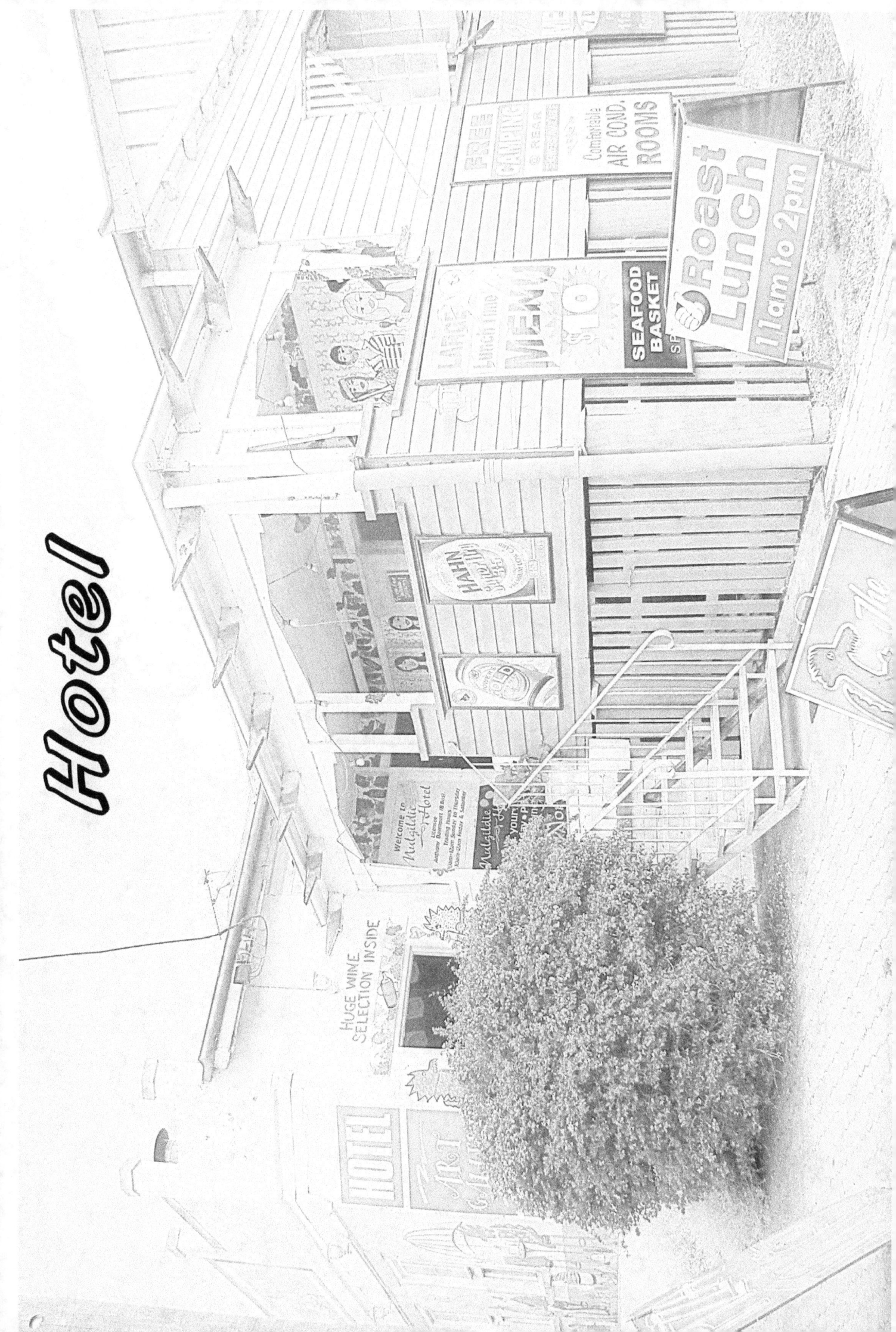

Hotel

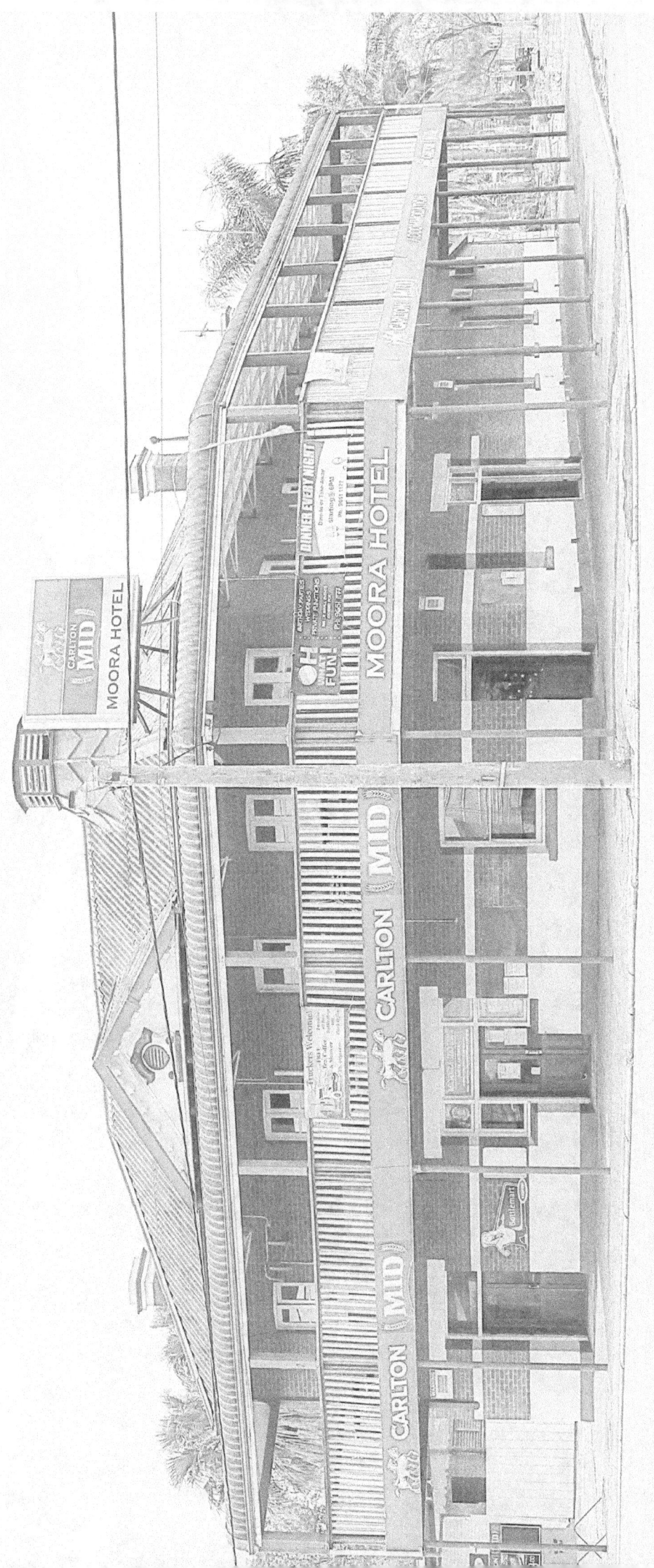

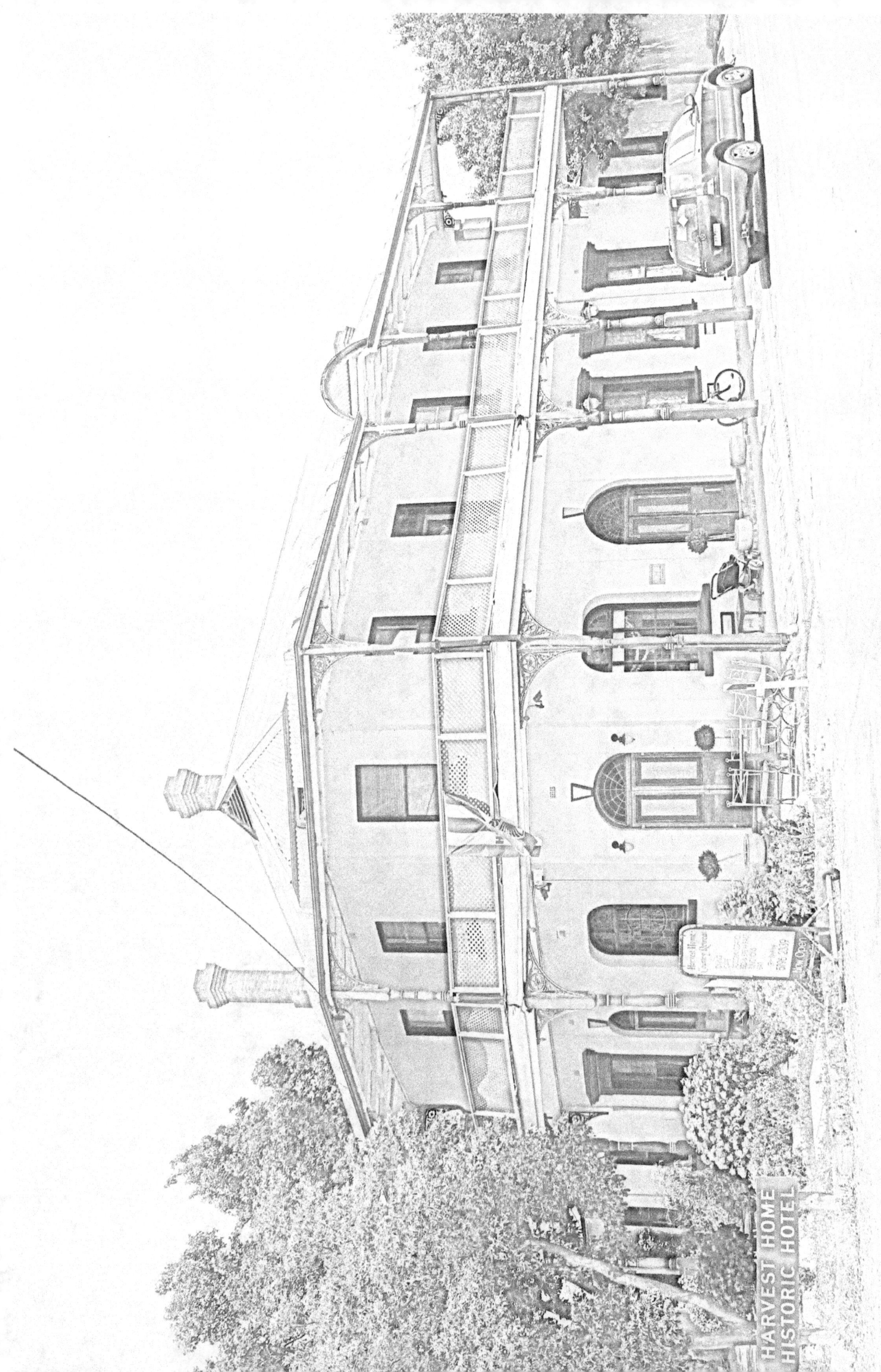

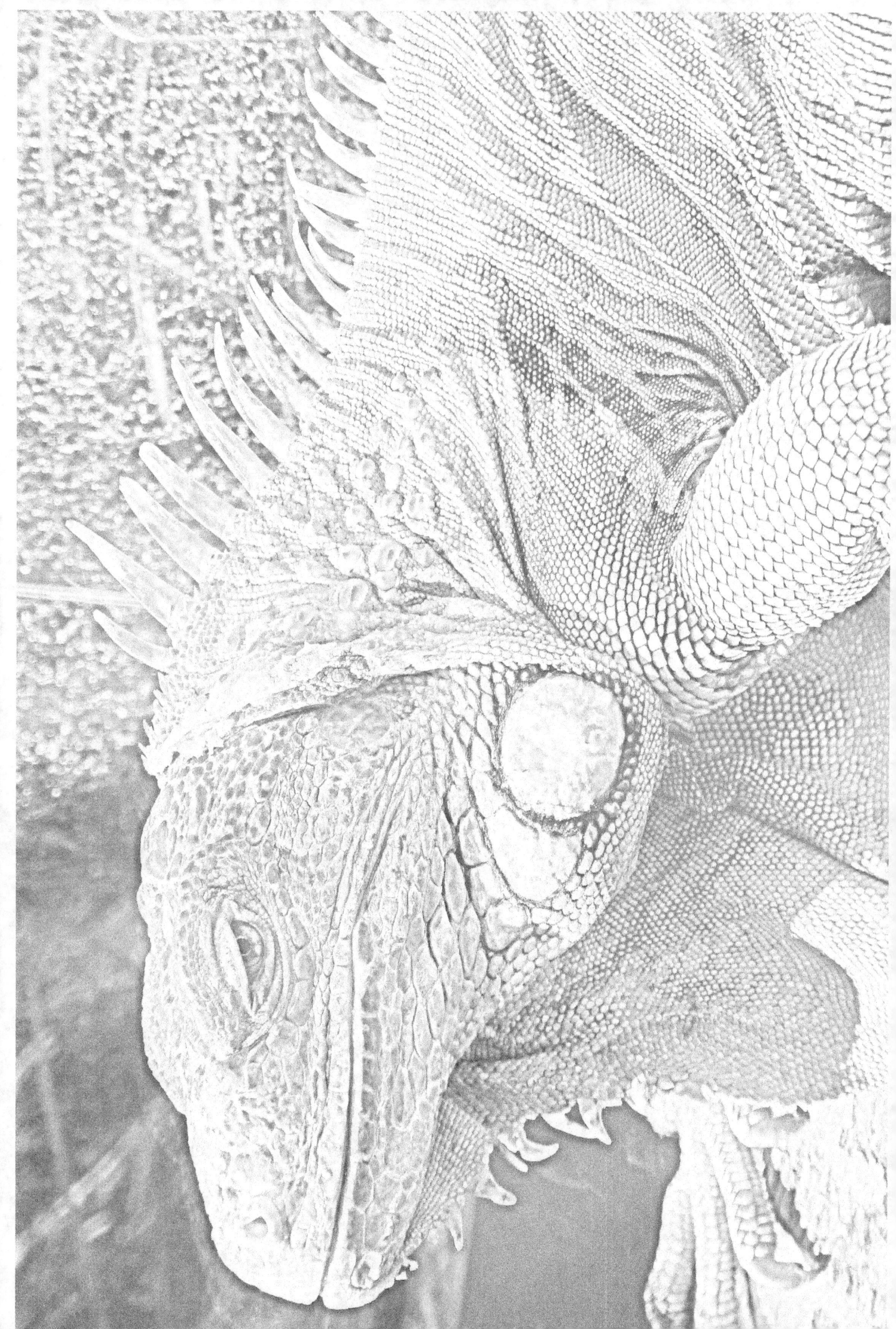

Lion

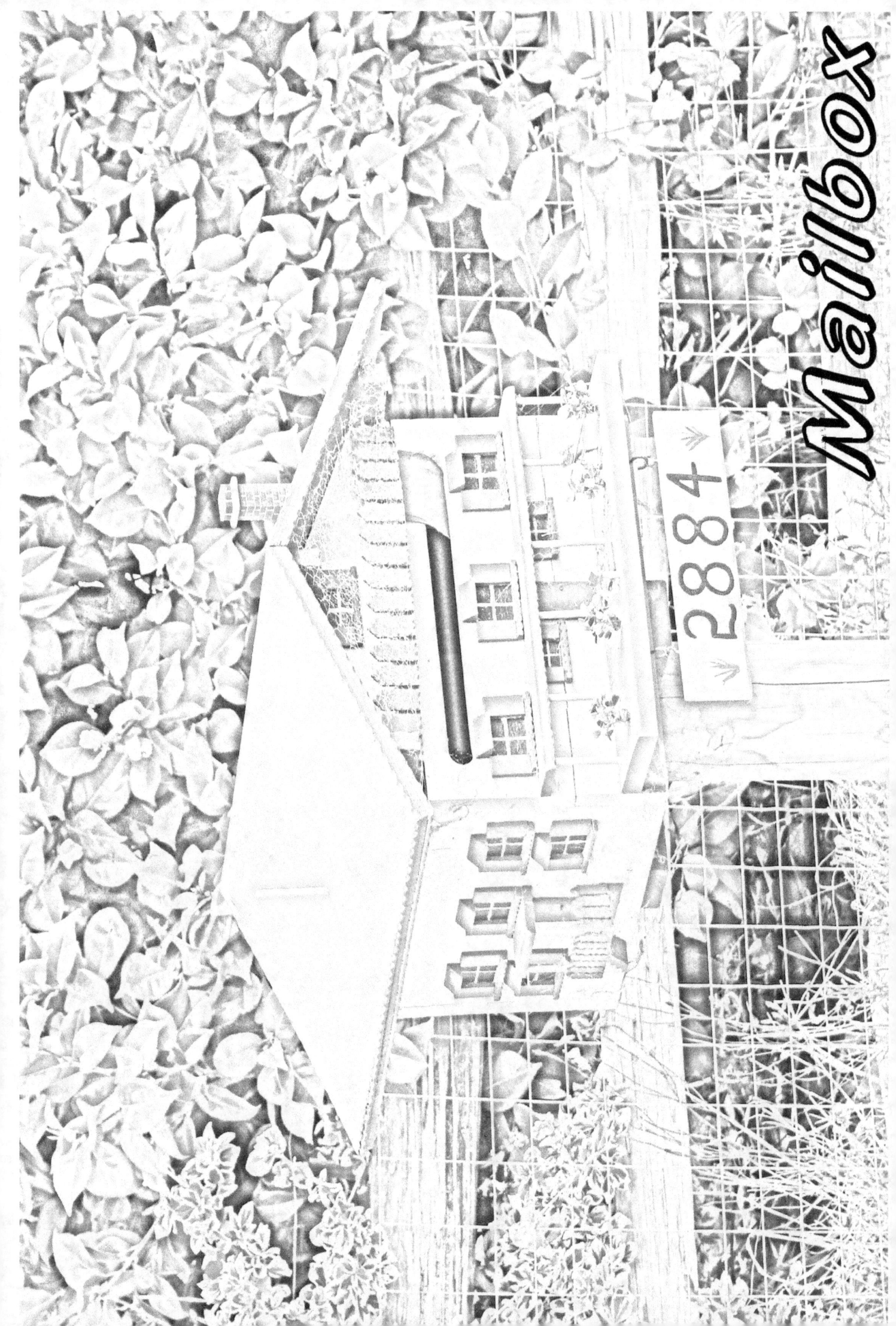

Mailbox

2884

Fire Station

FIRE STATION

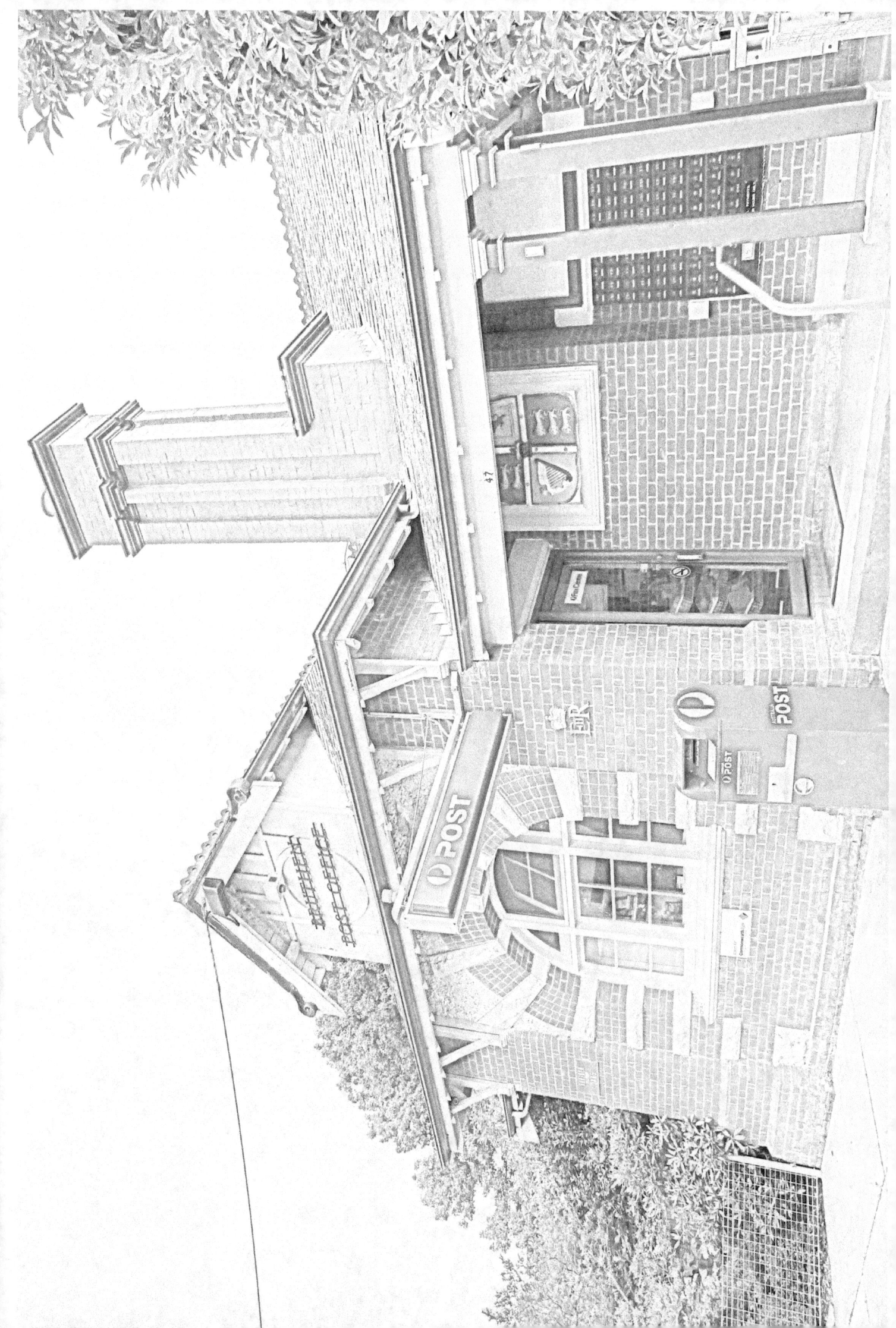

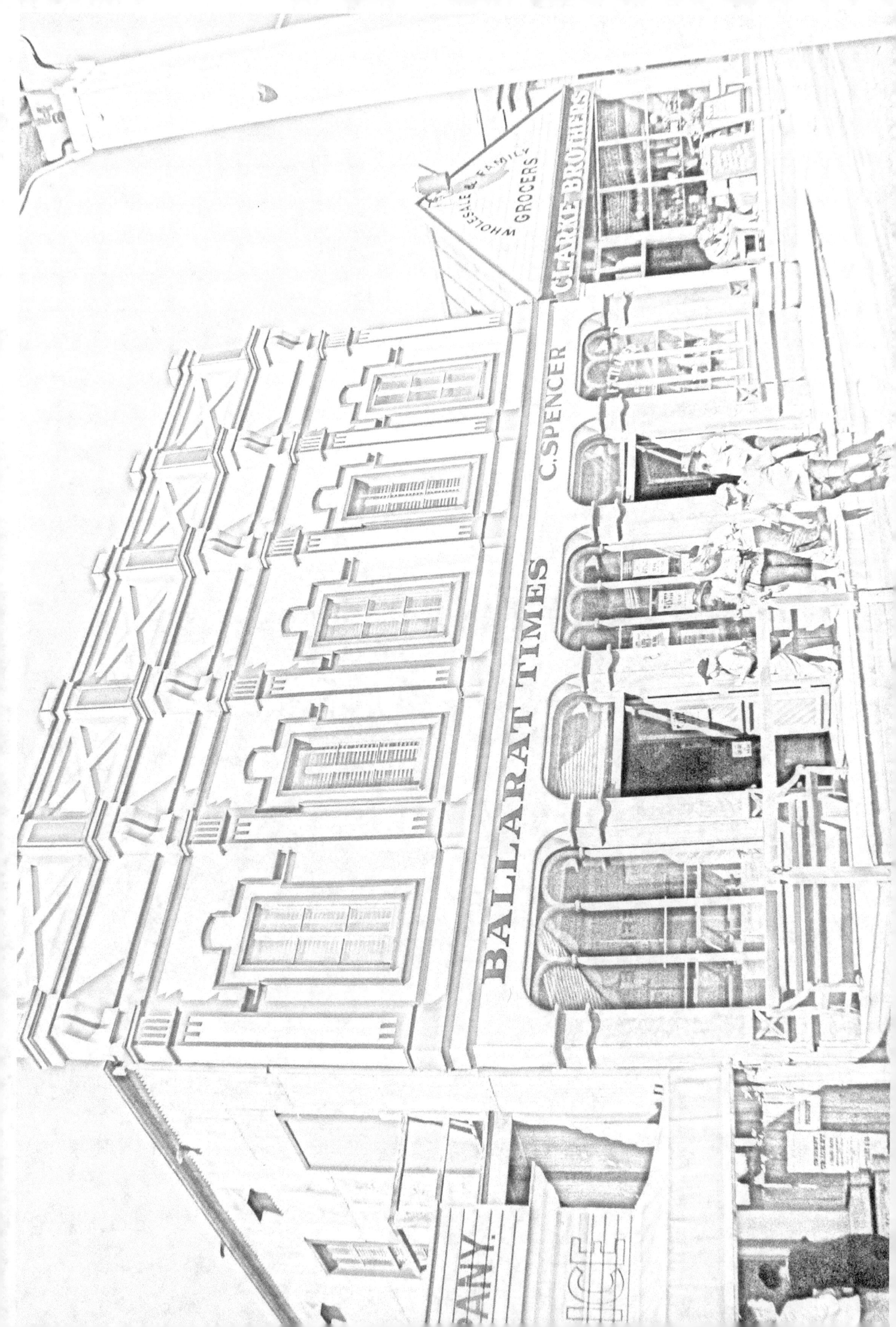

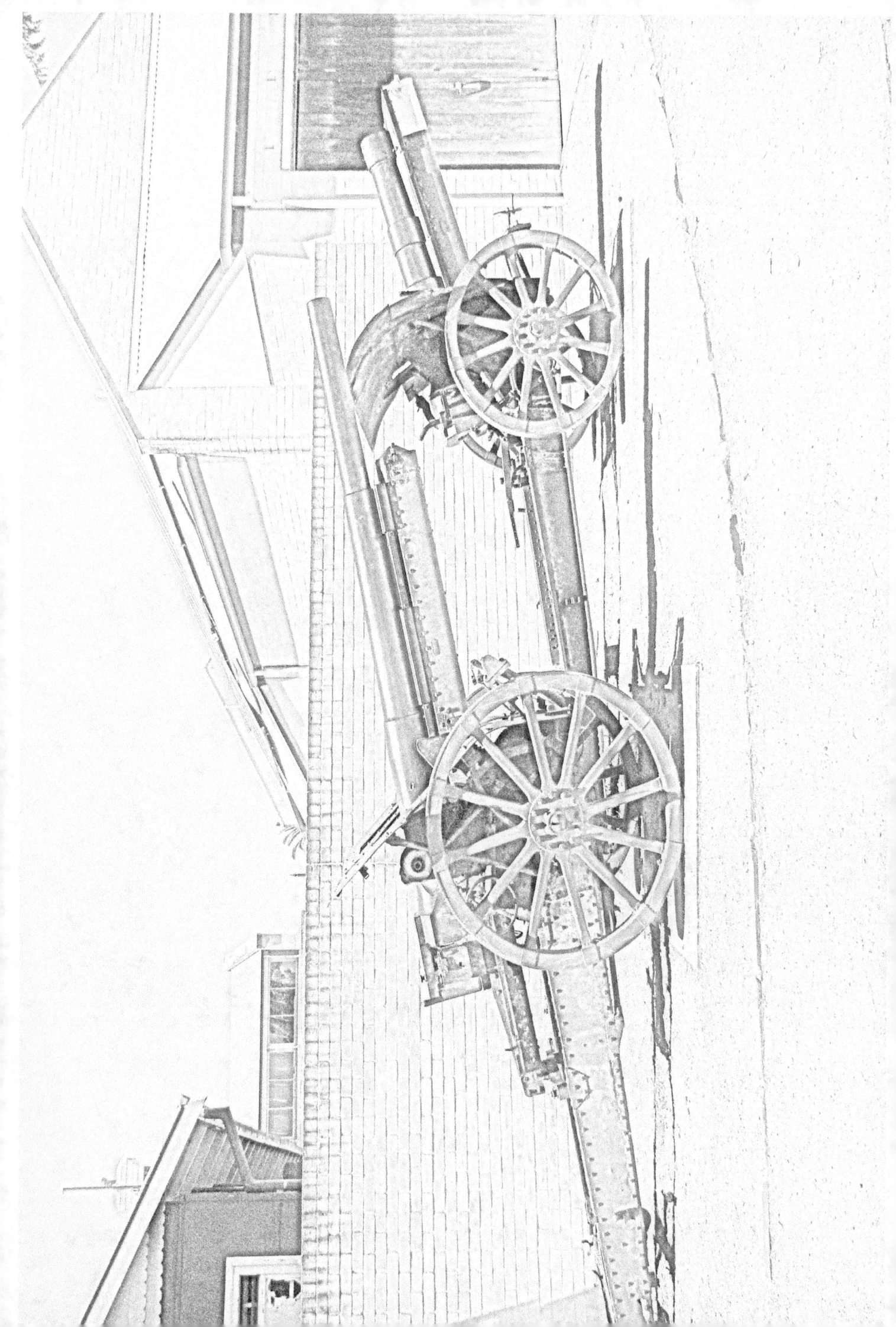

Rosella

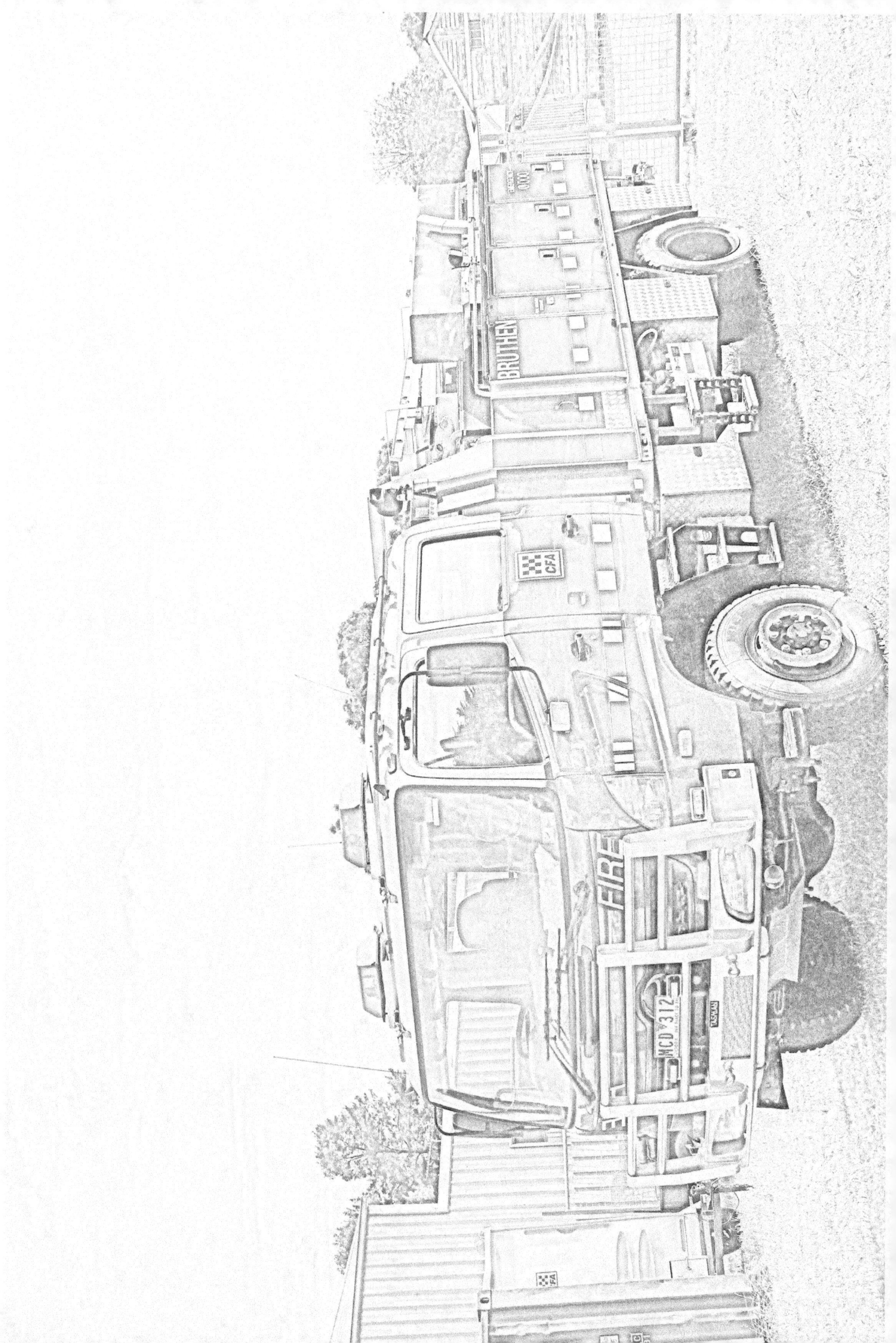

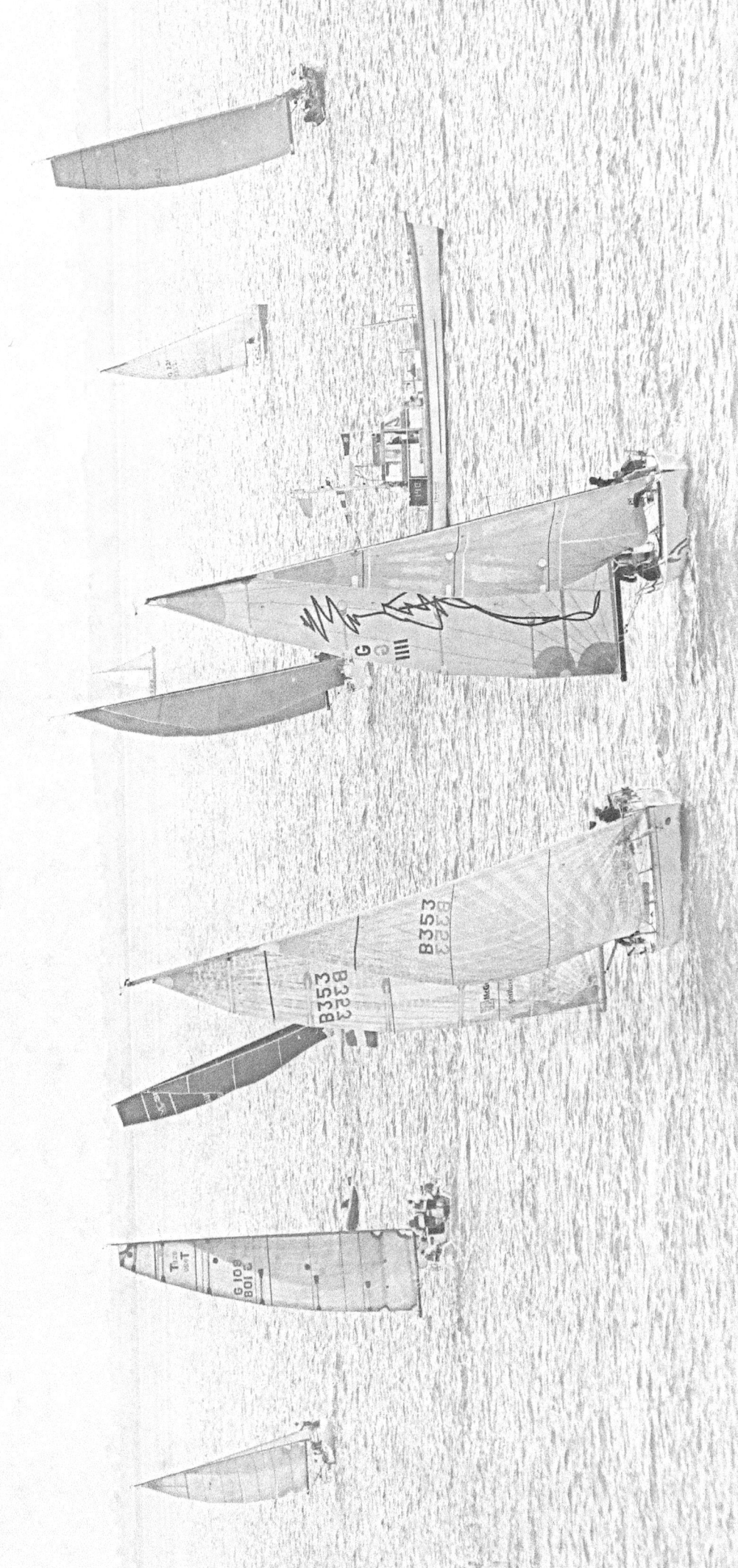

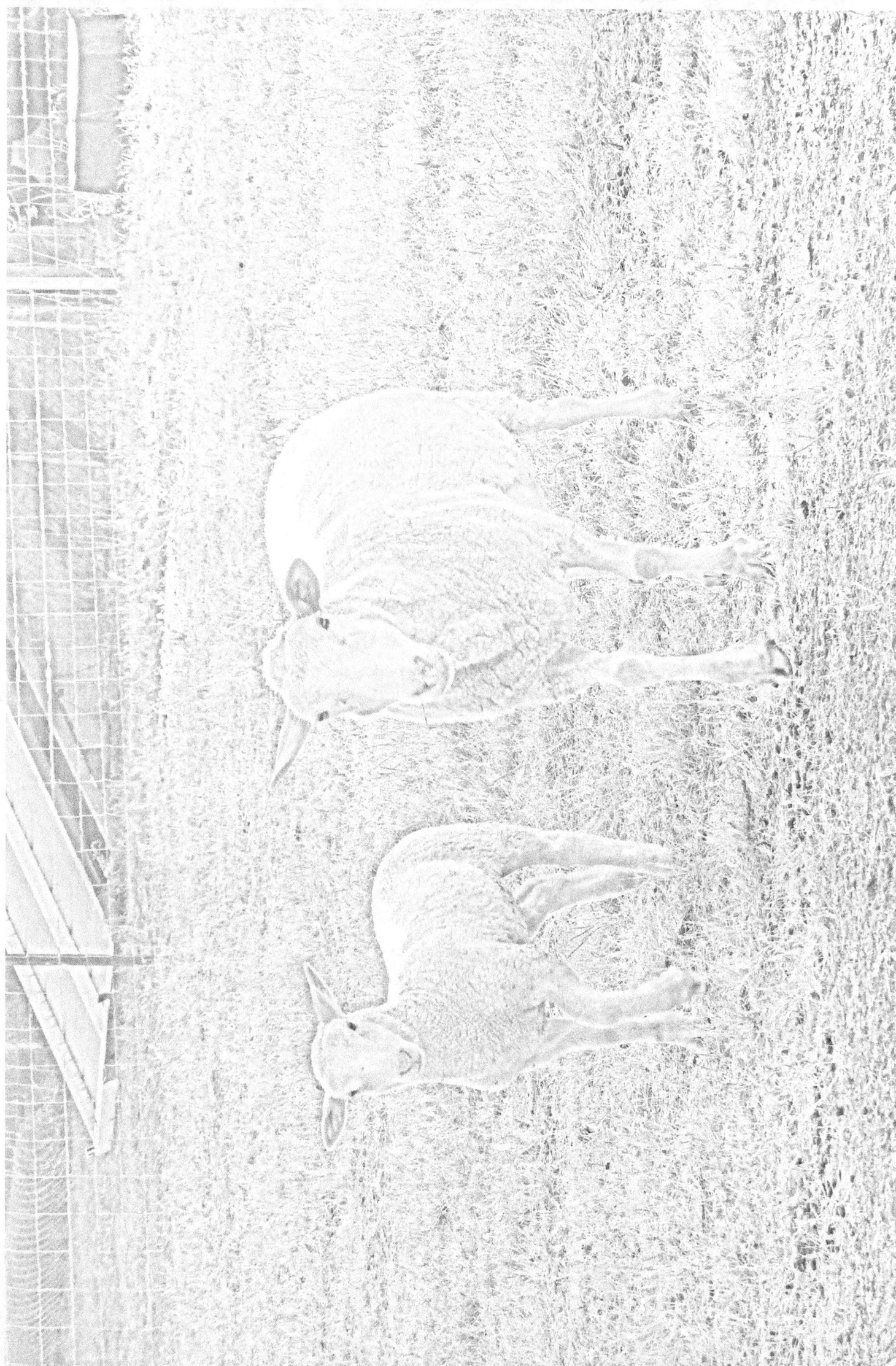

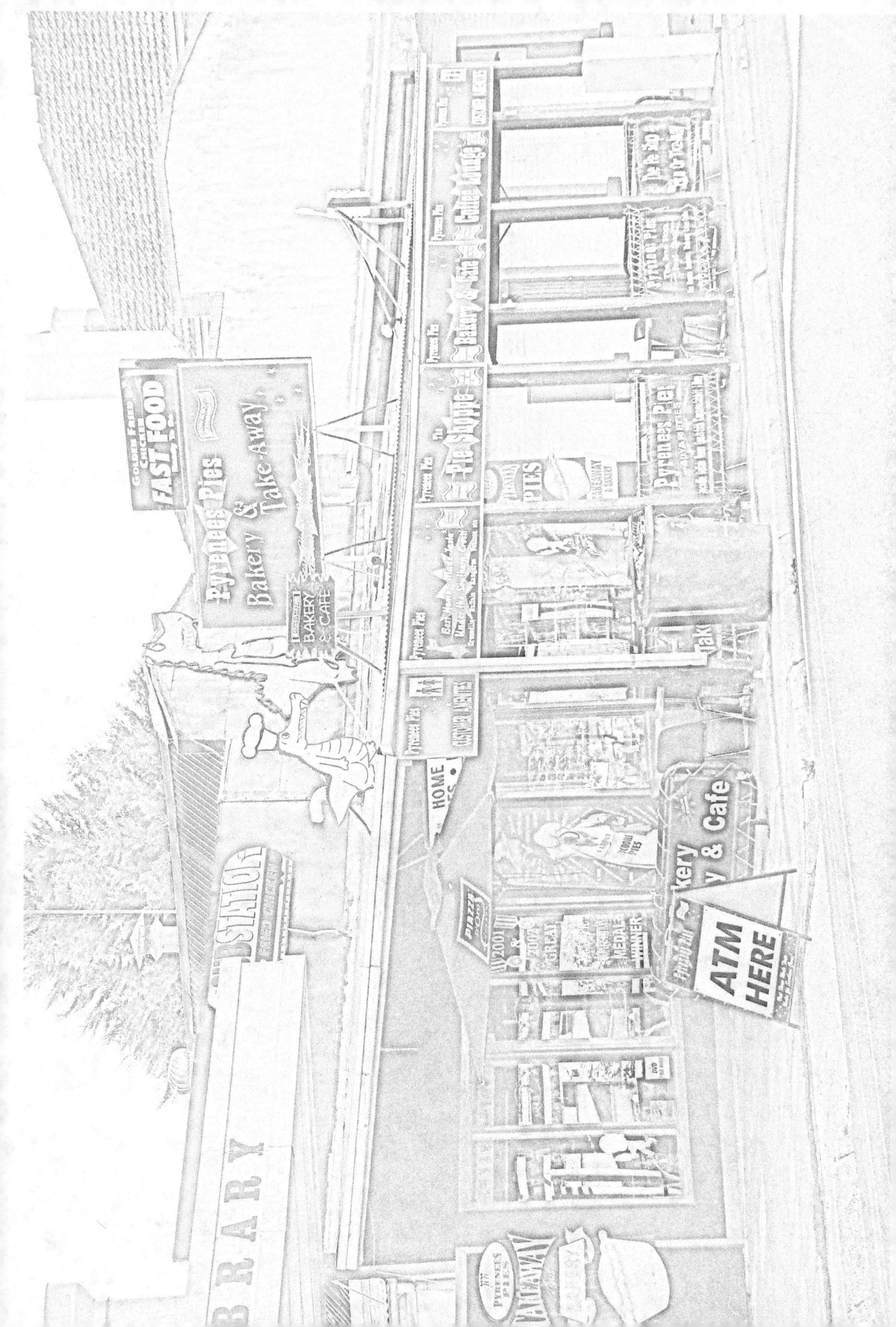

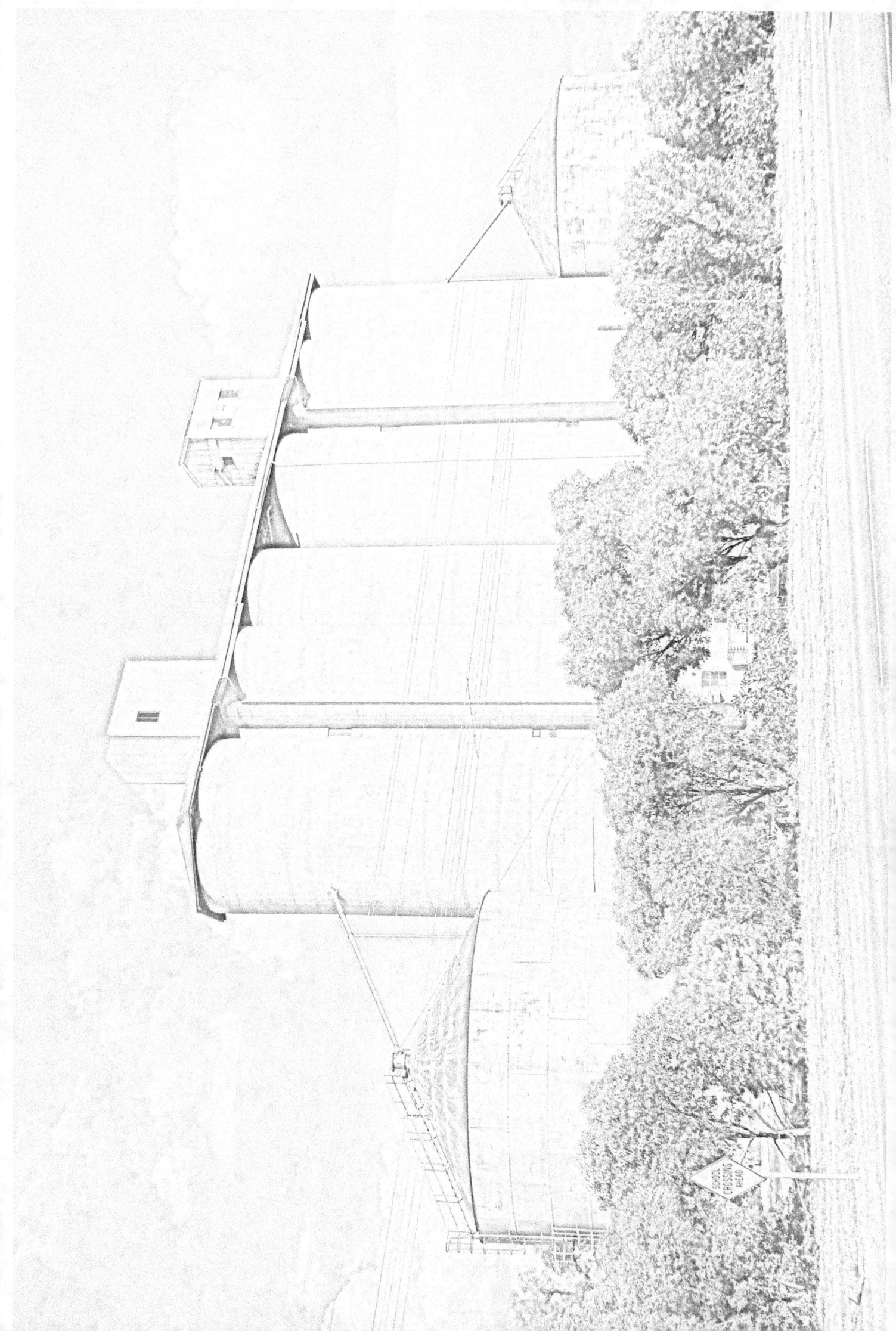

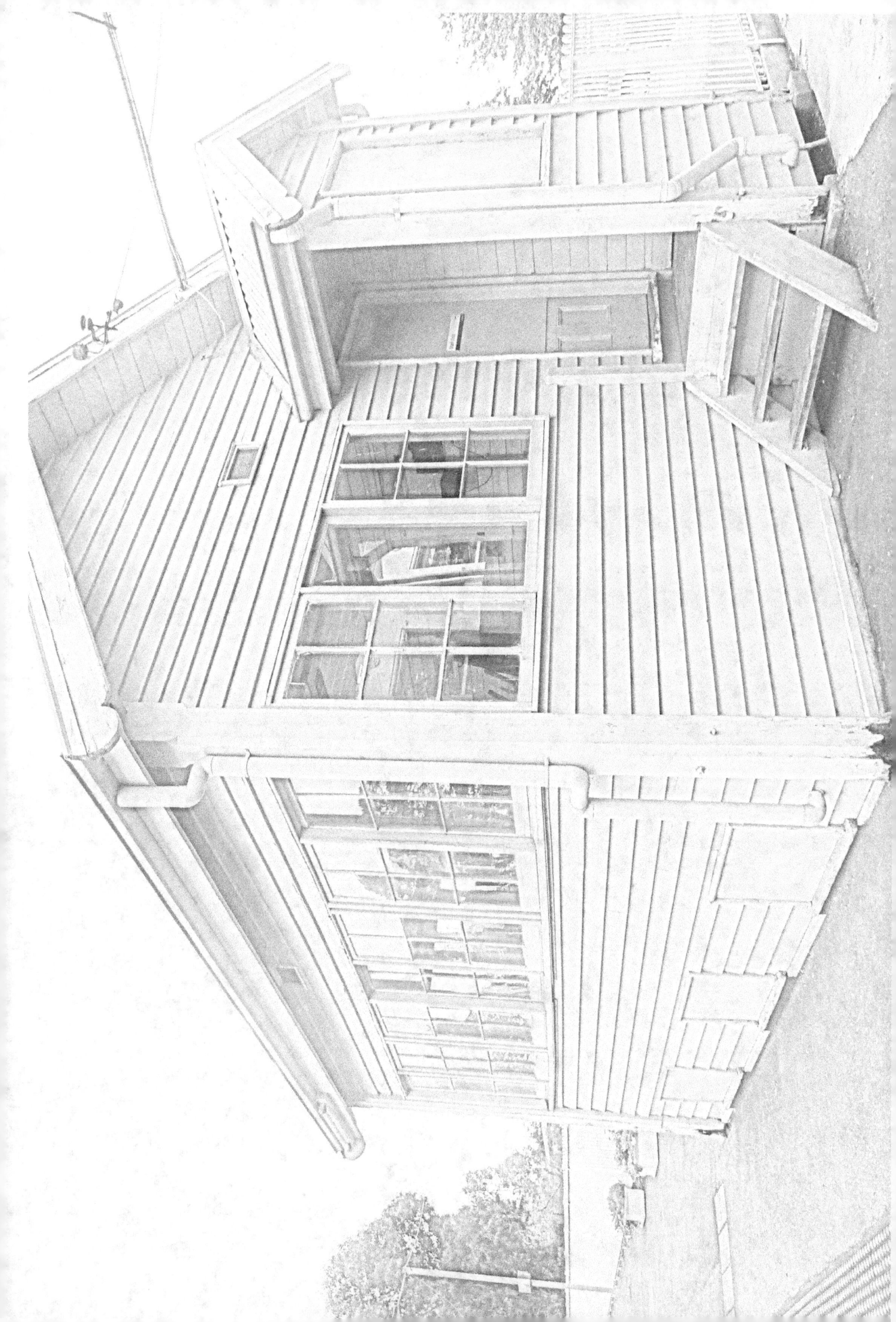

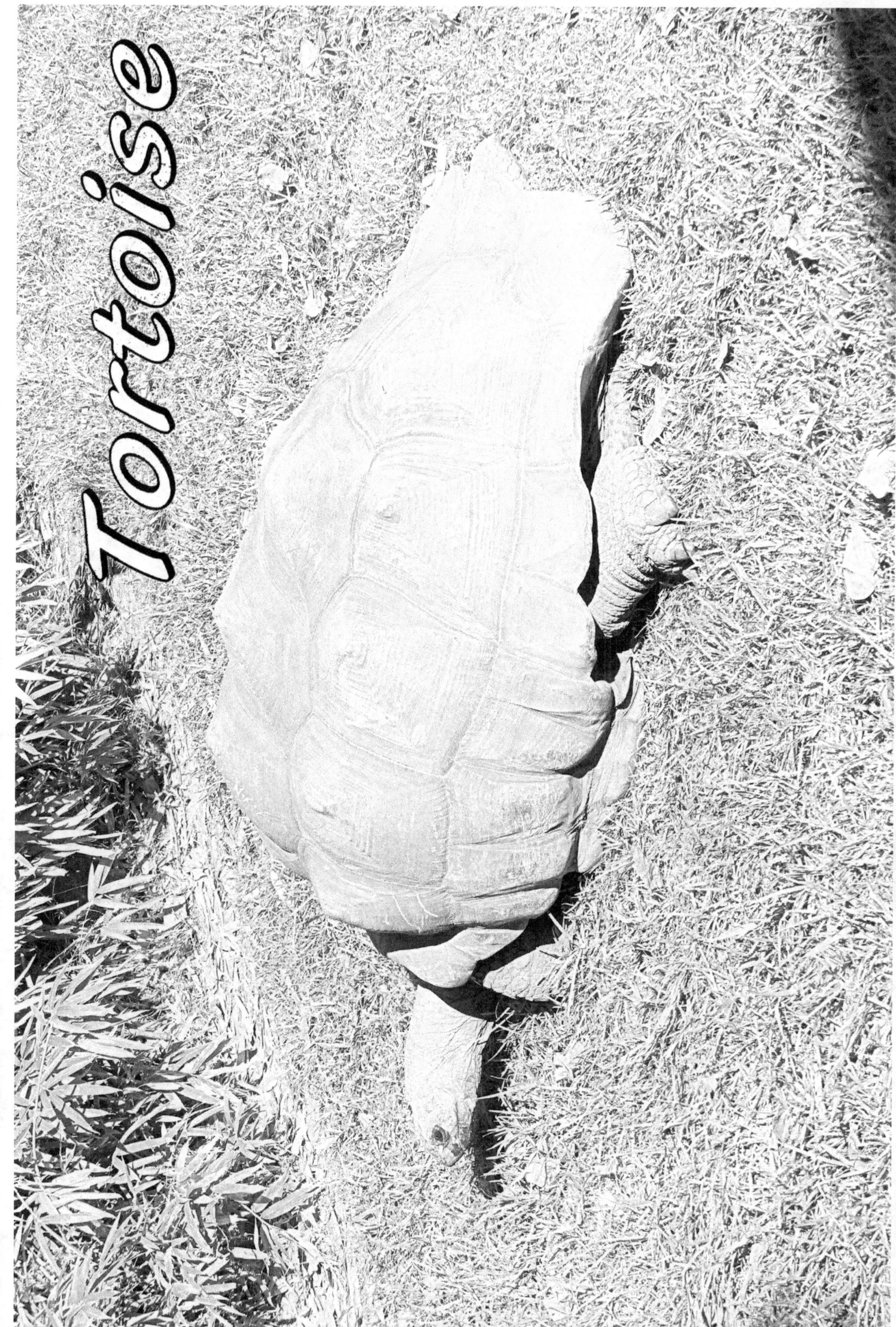

Tortoise

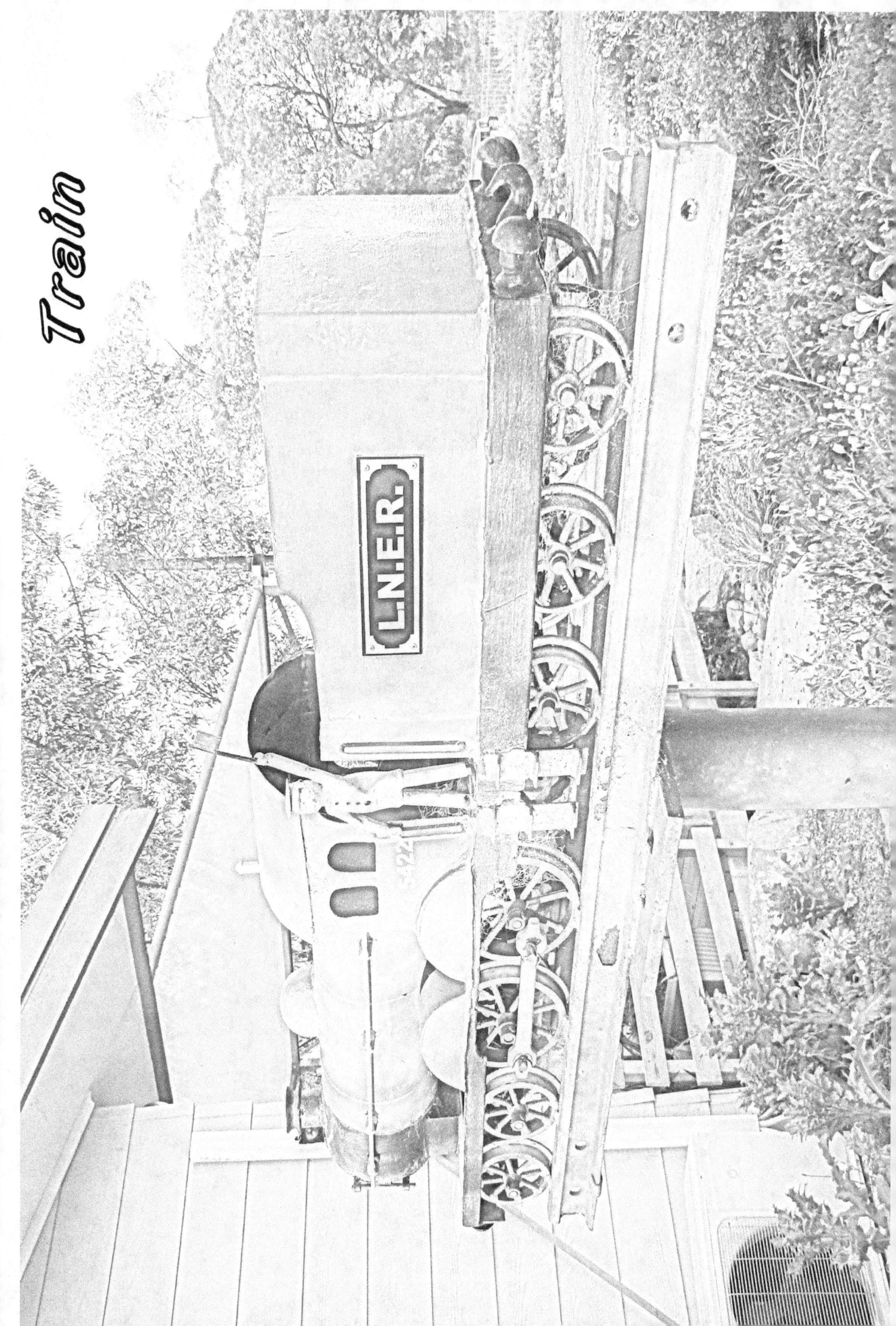

Train

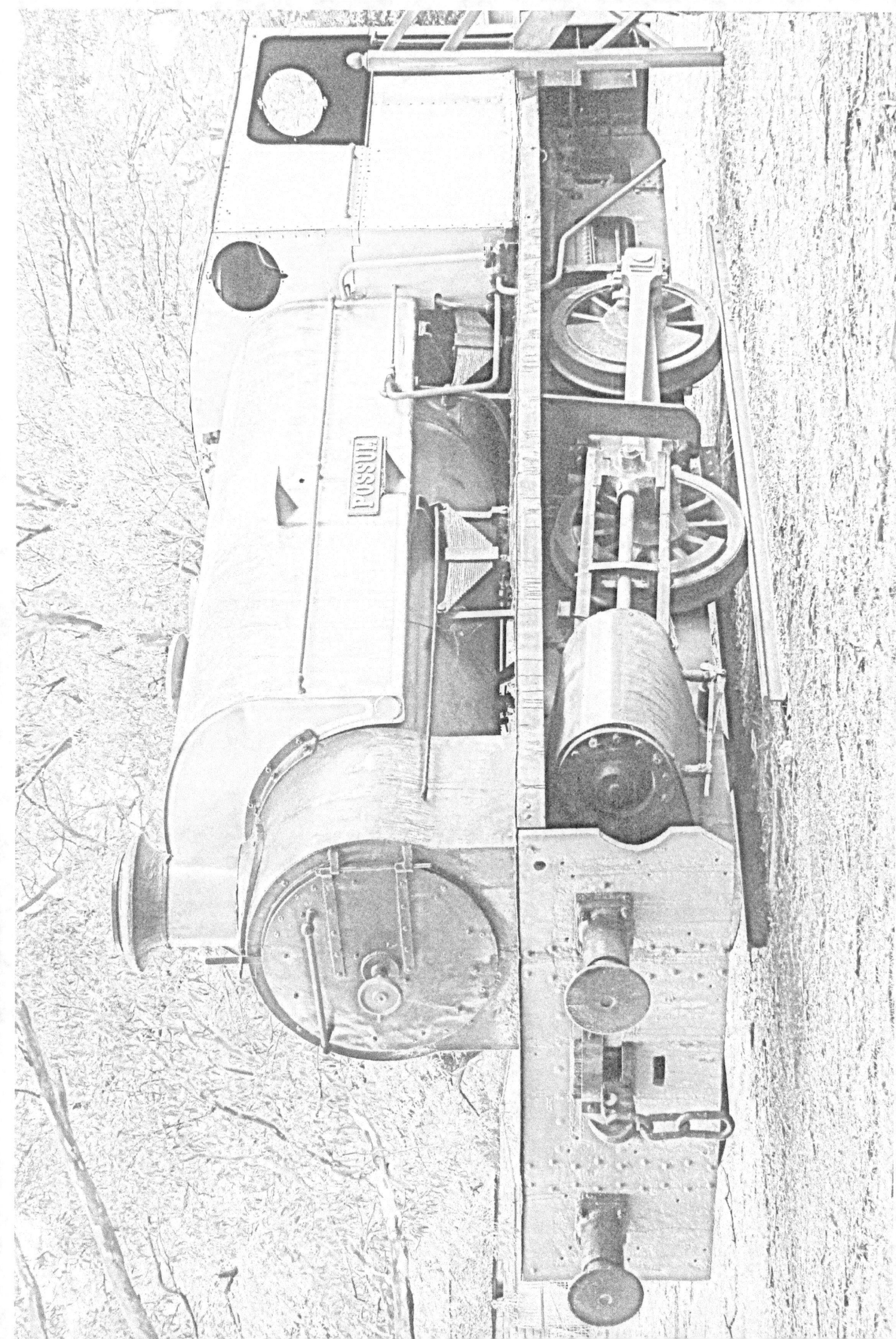

Tram

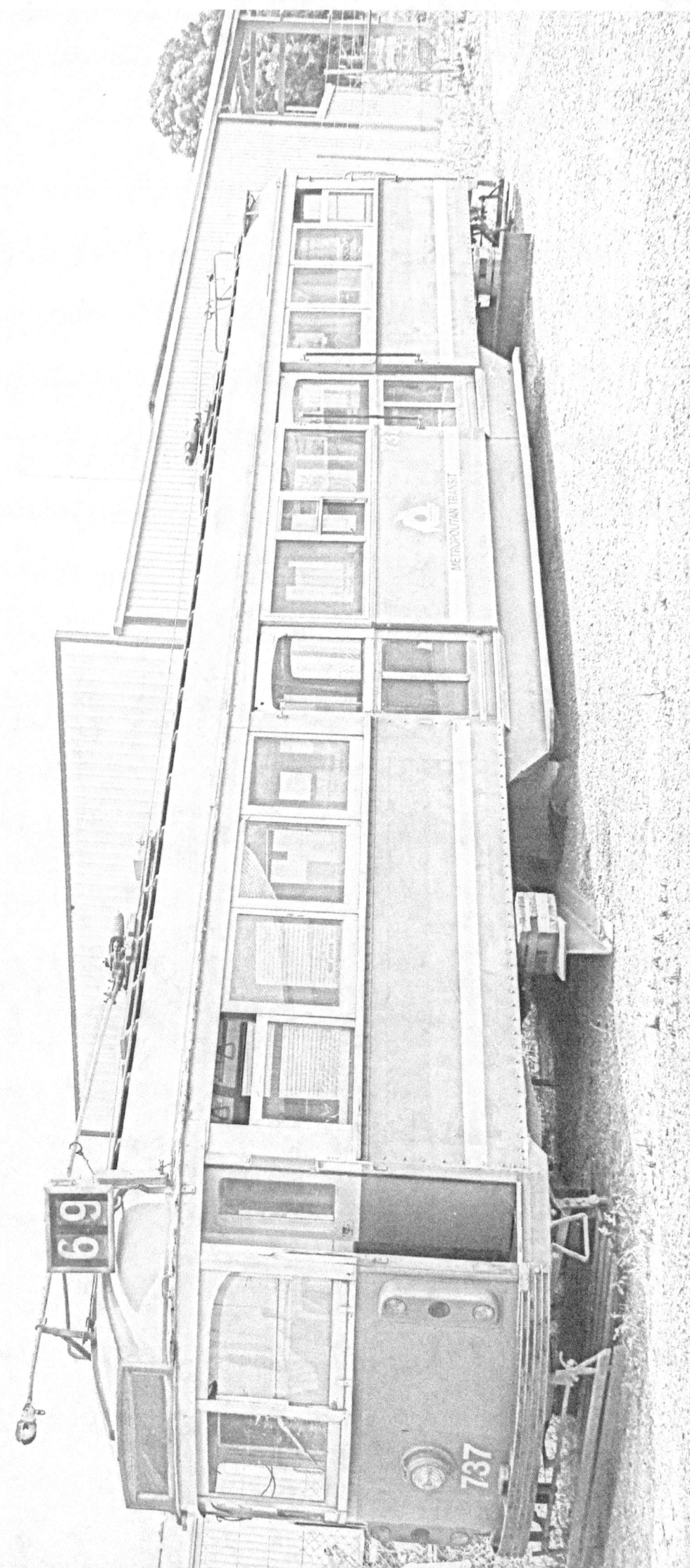

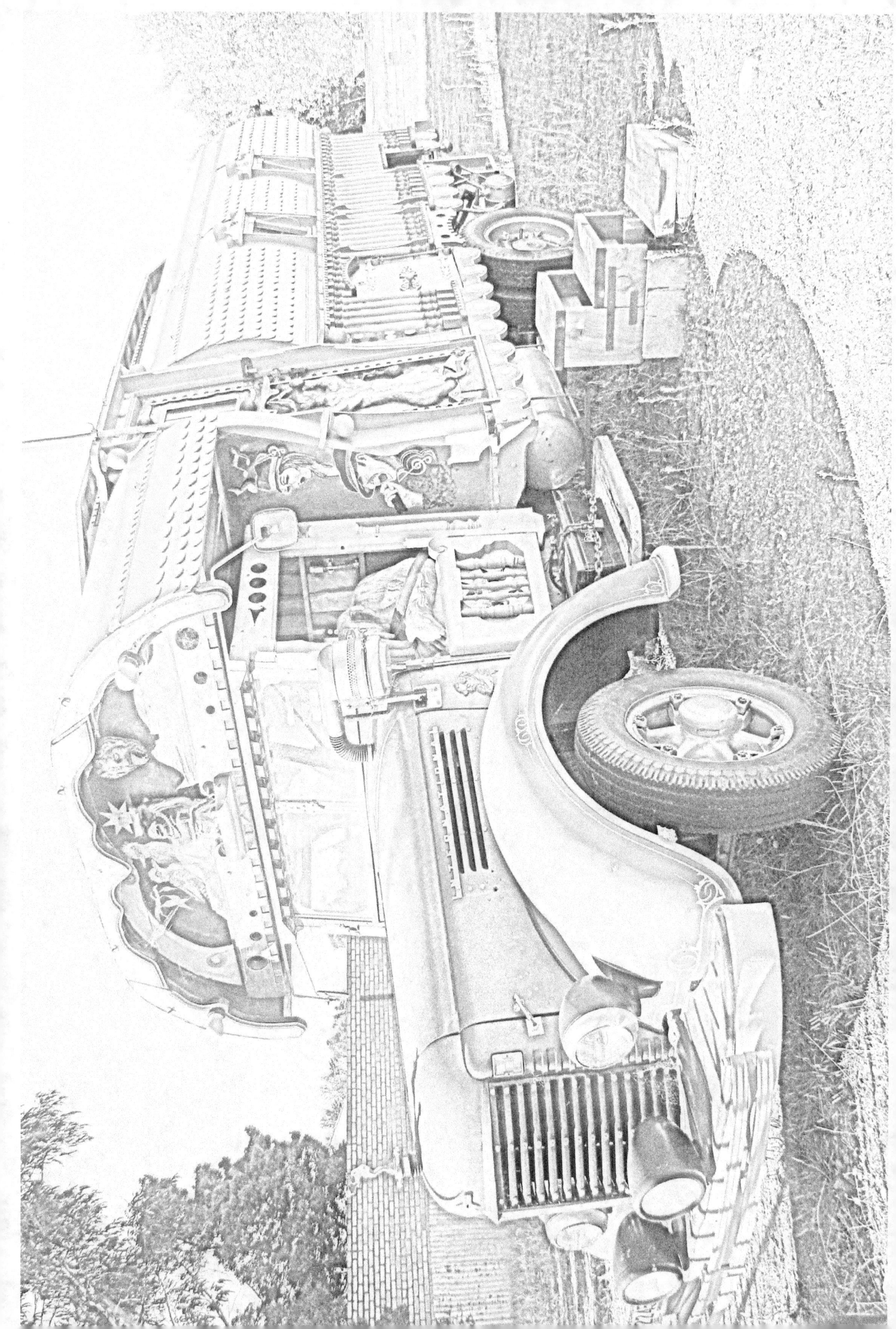

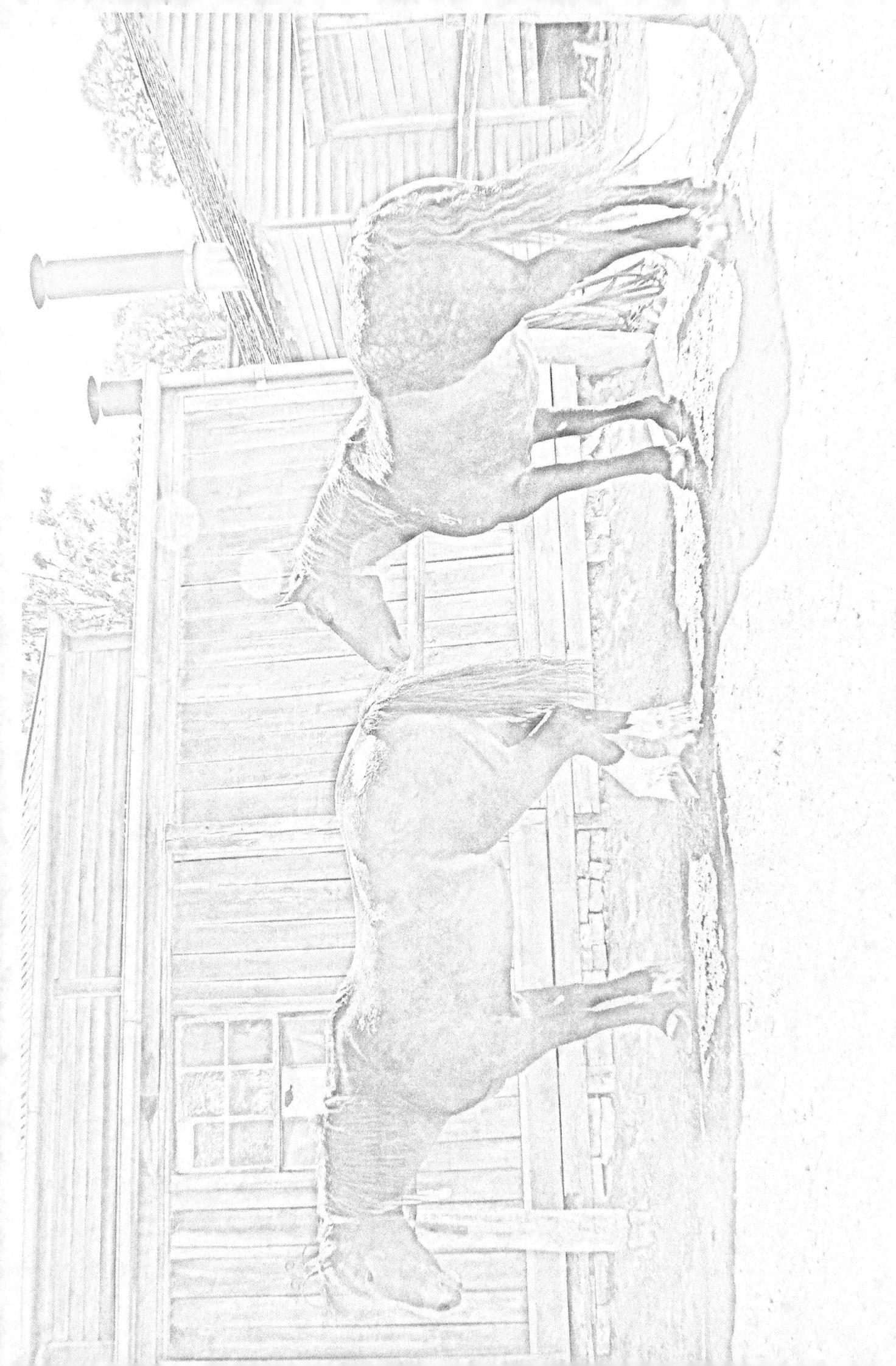

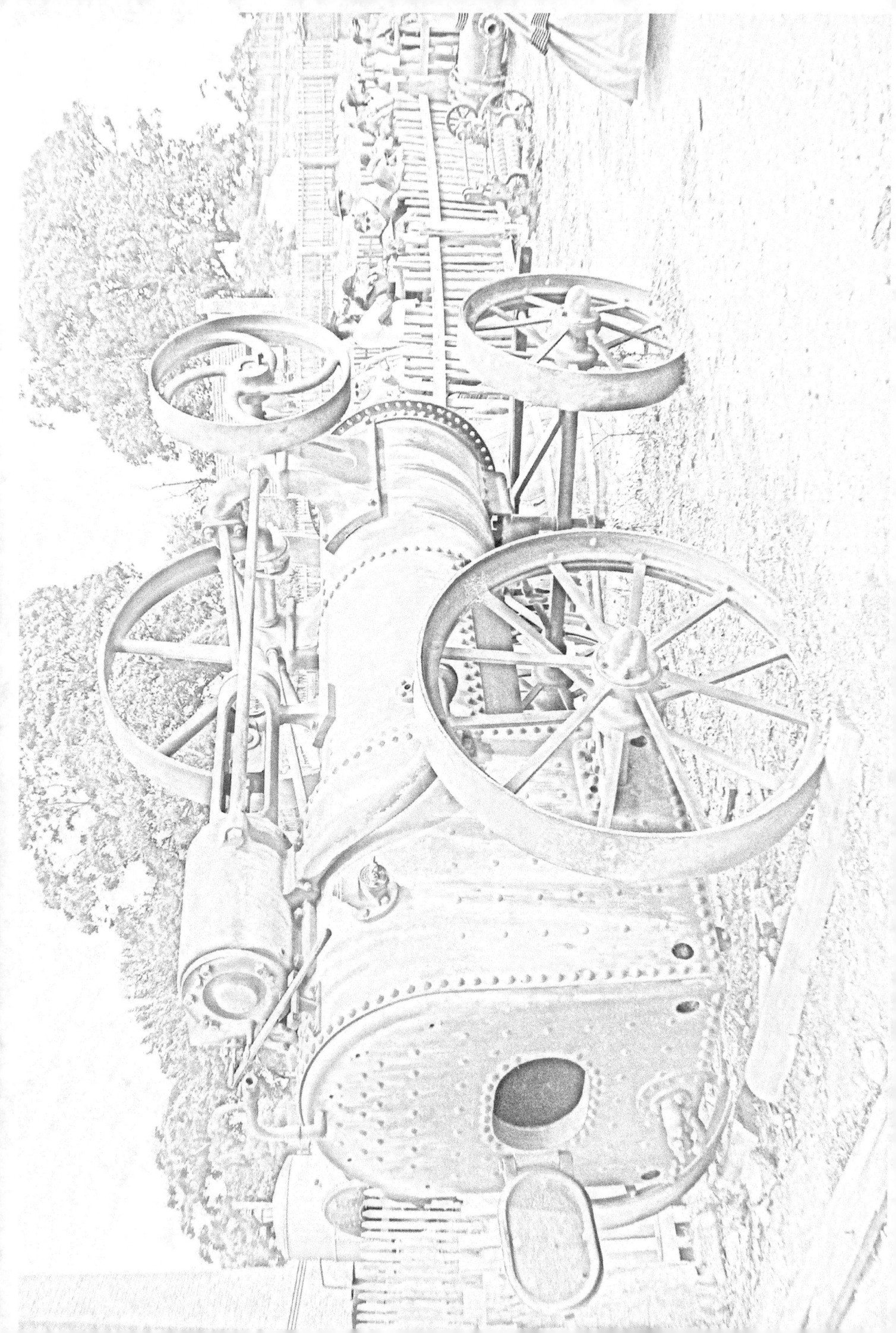

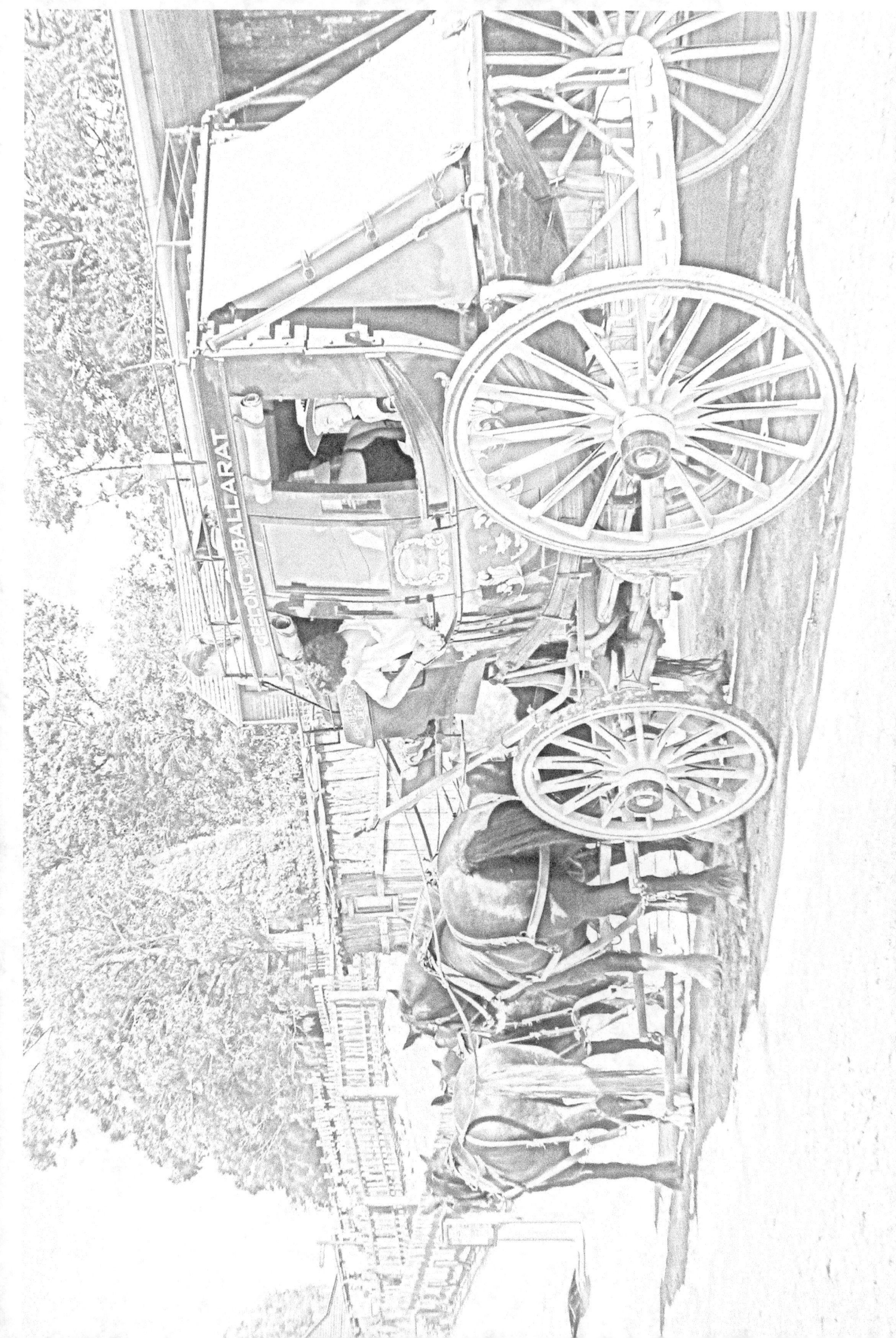

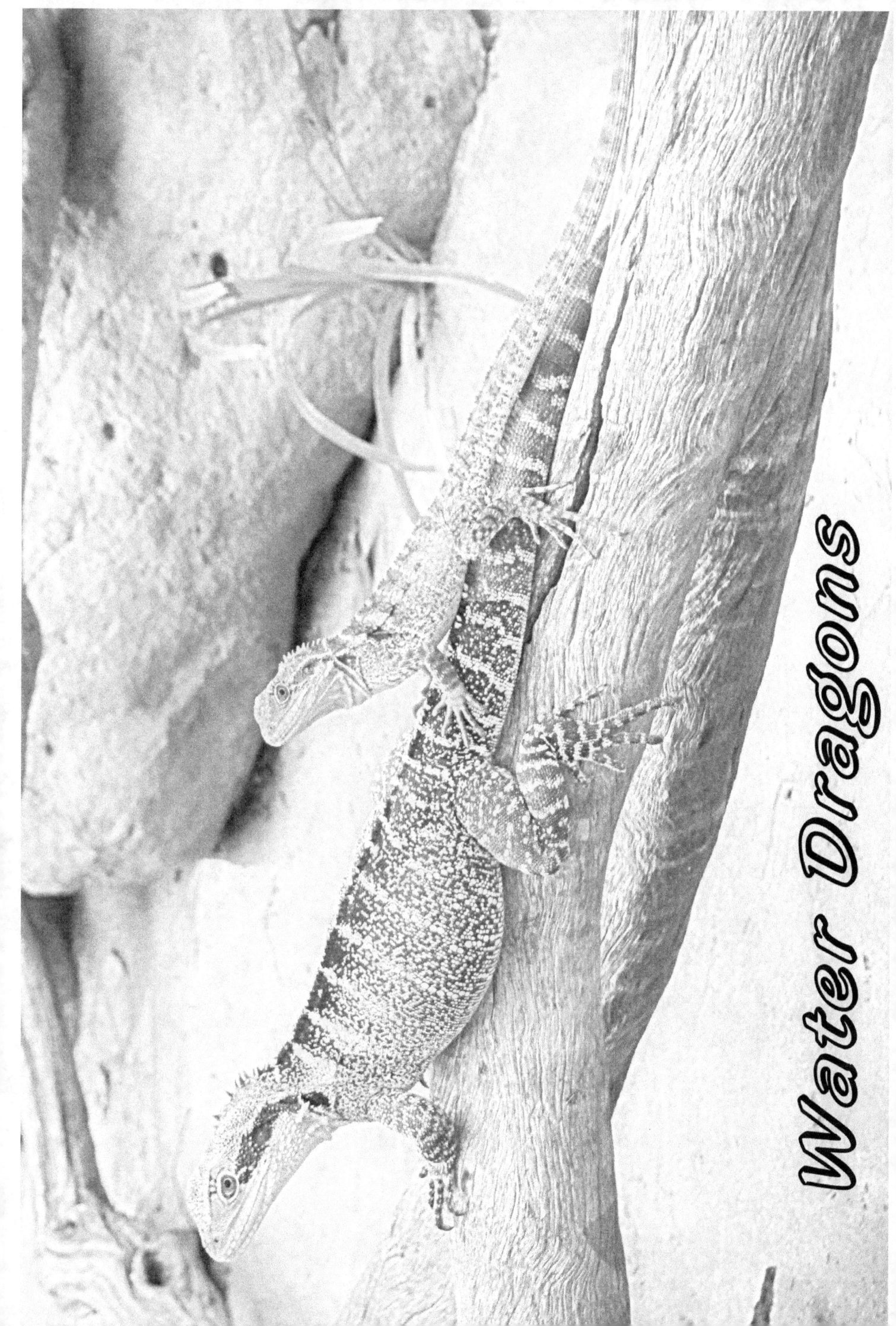

Water Dragons

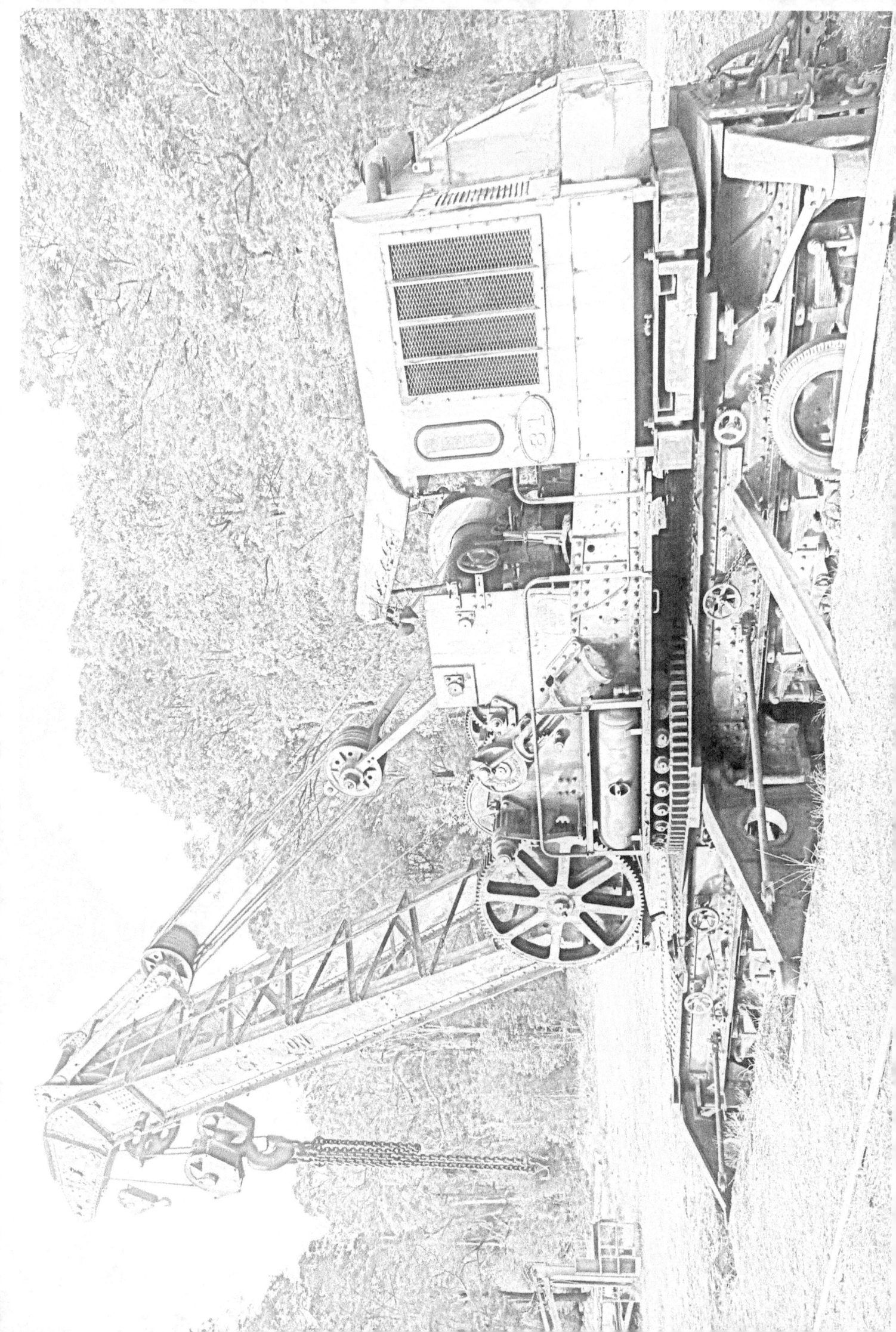

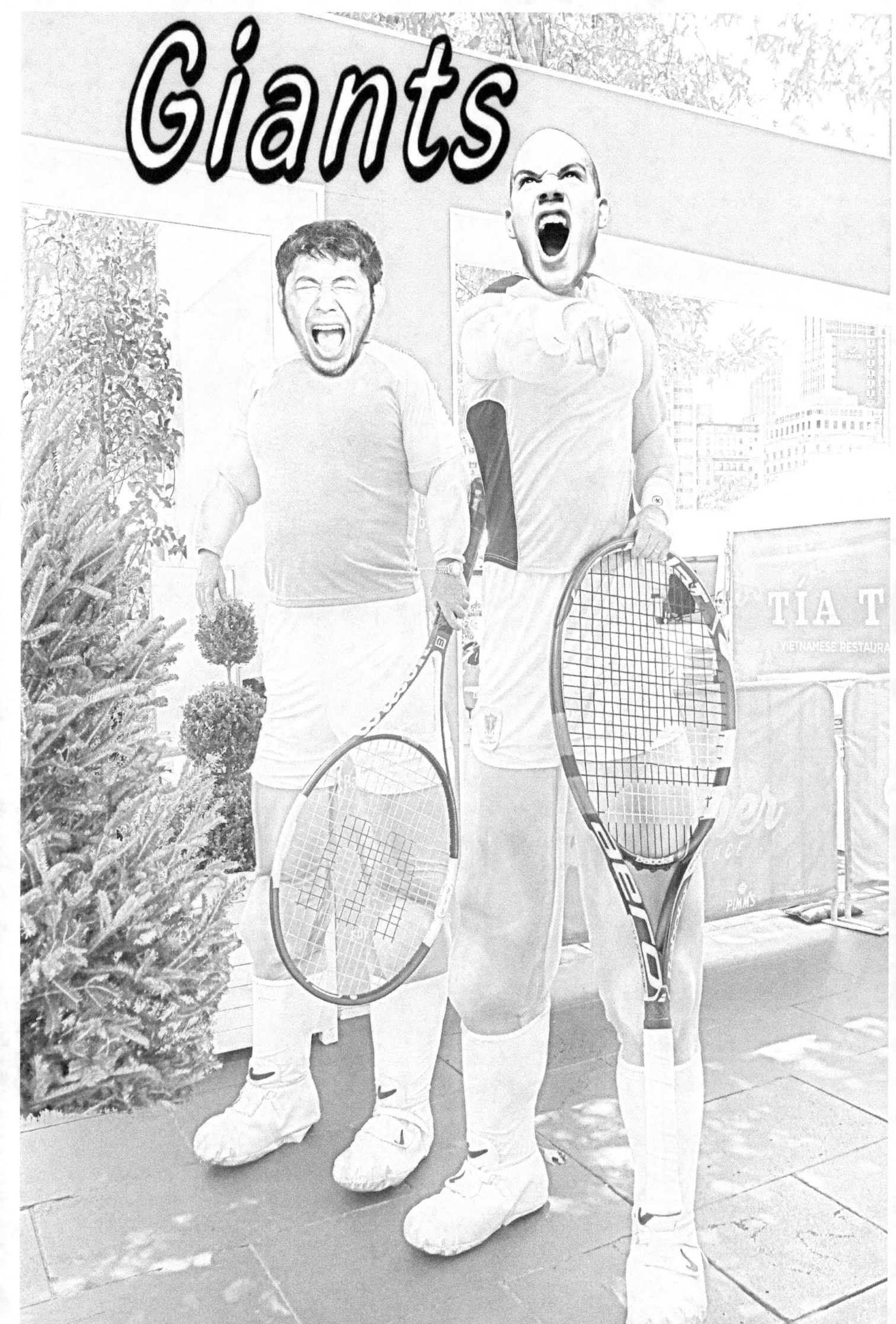

Big
Gold
Panner

GOLD PANNER
MOTOR

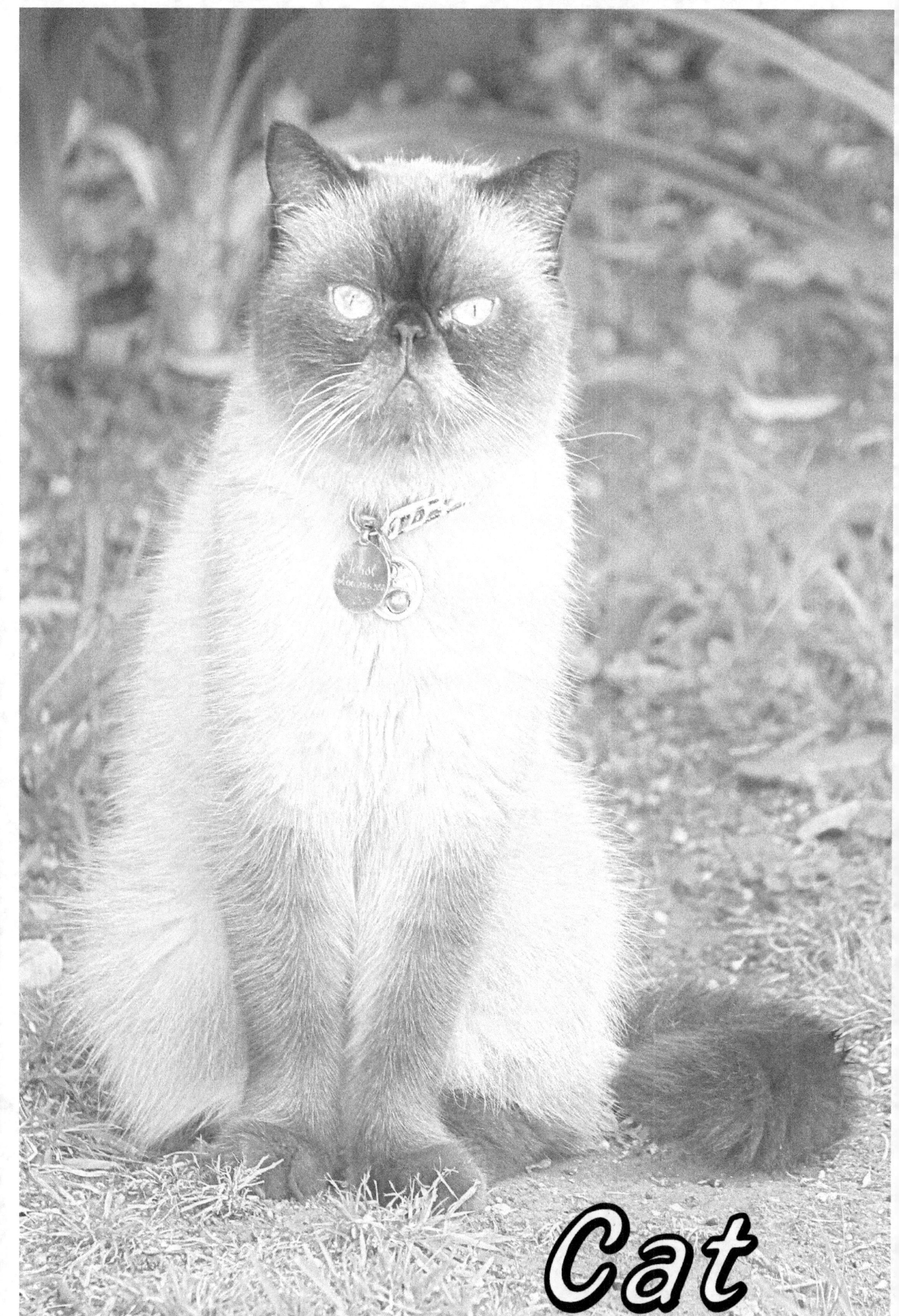

Cat

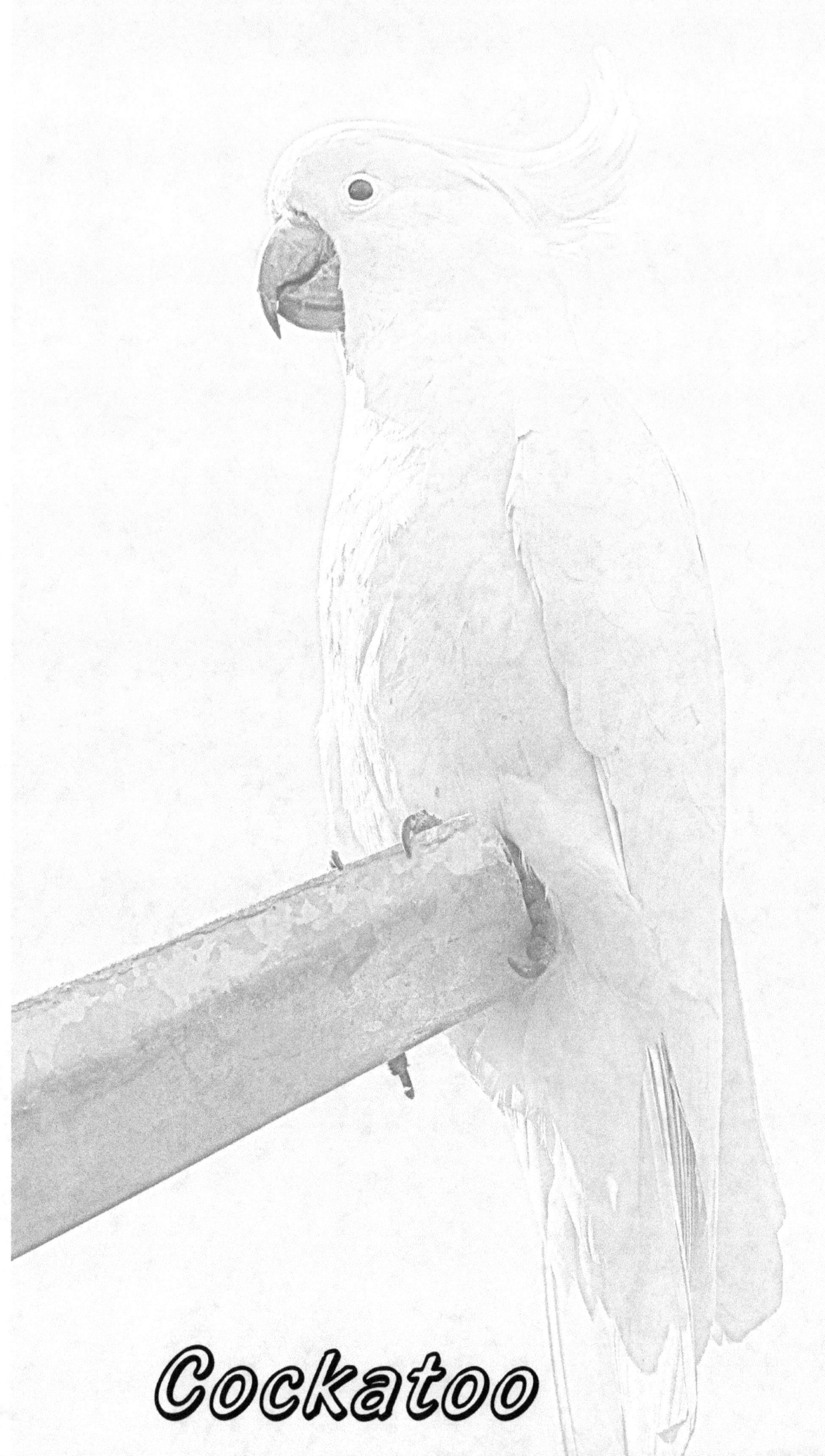

Cockatoo

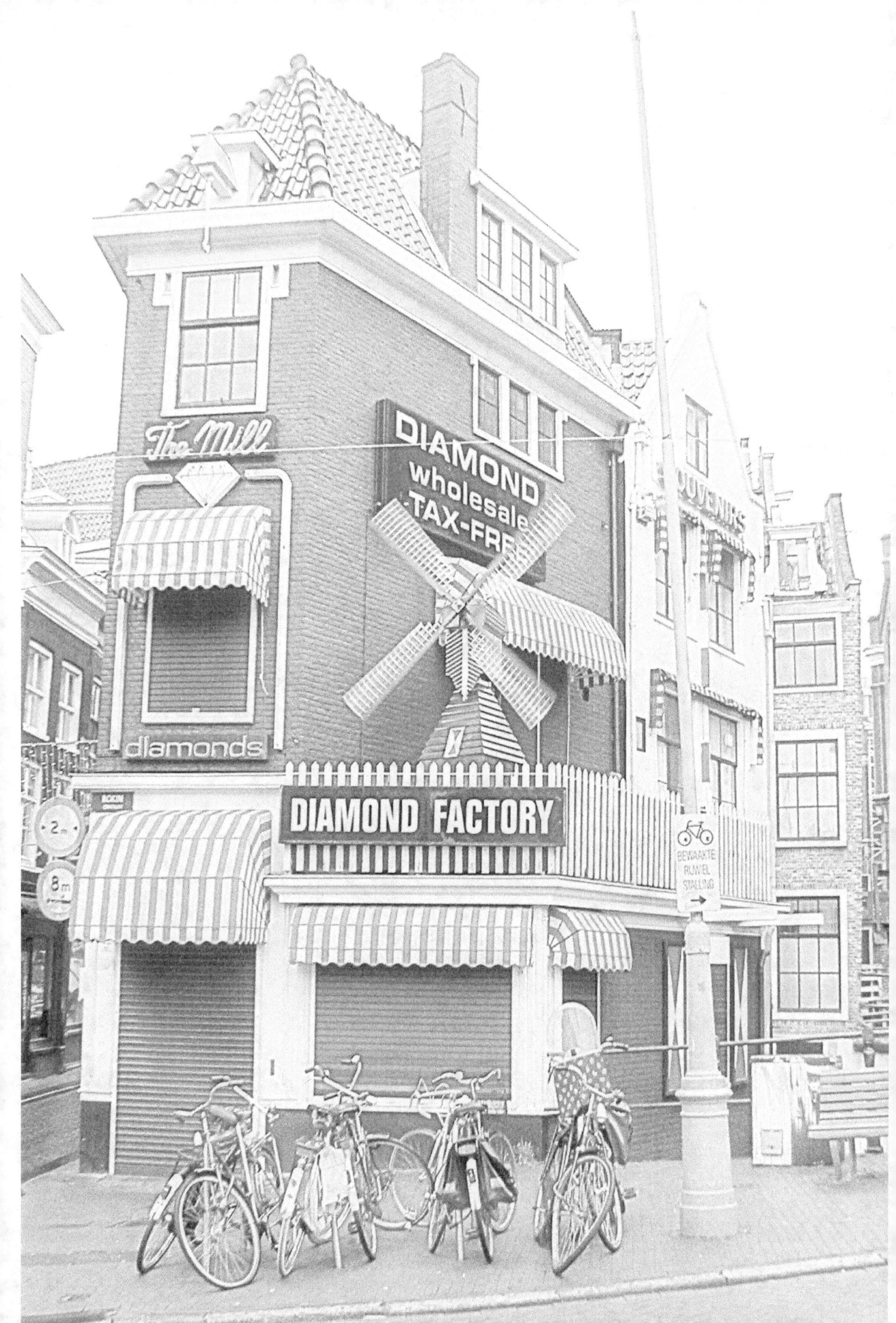

Koala

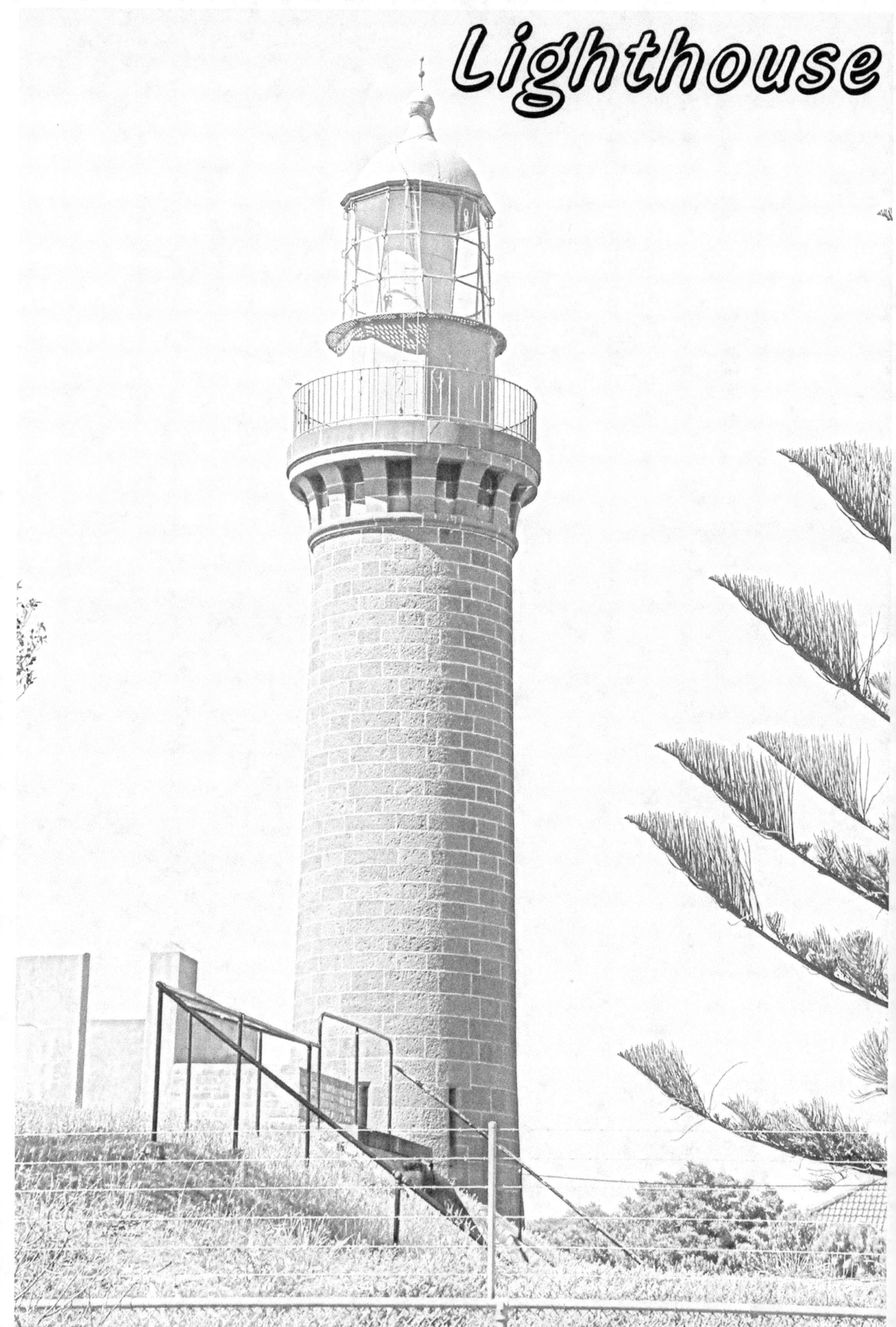

Lighthouse

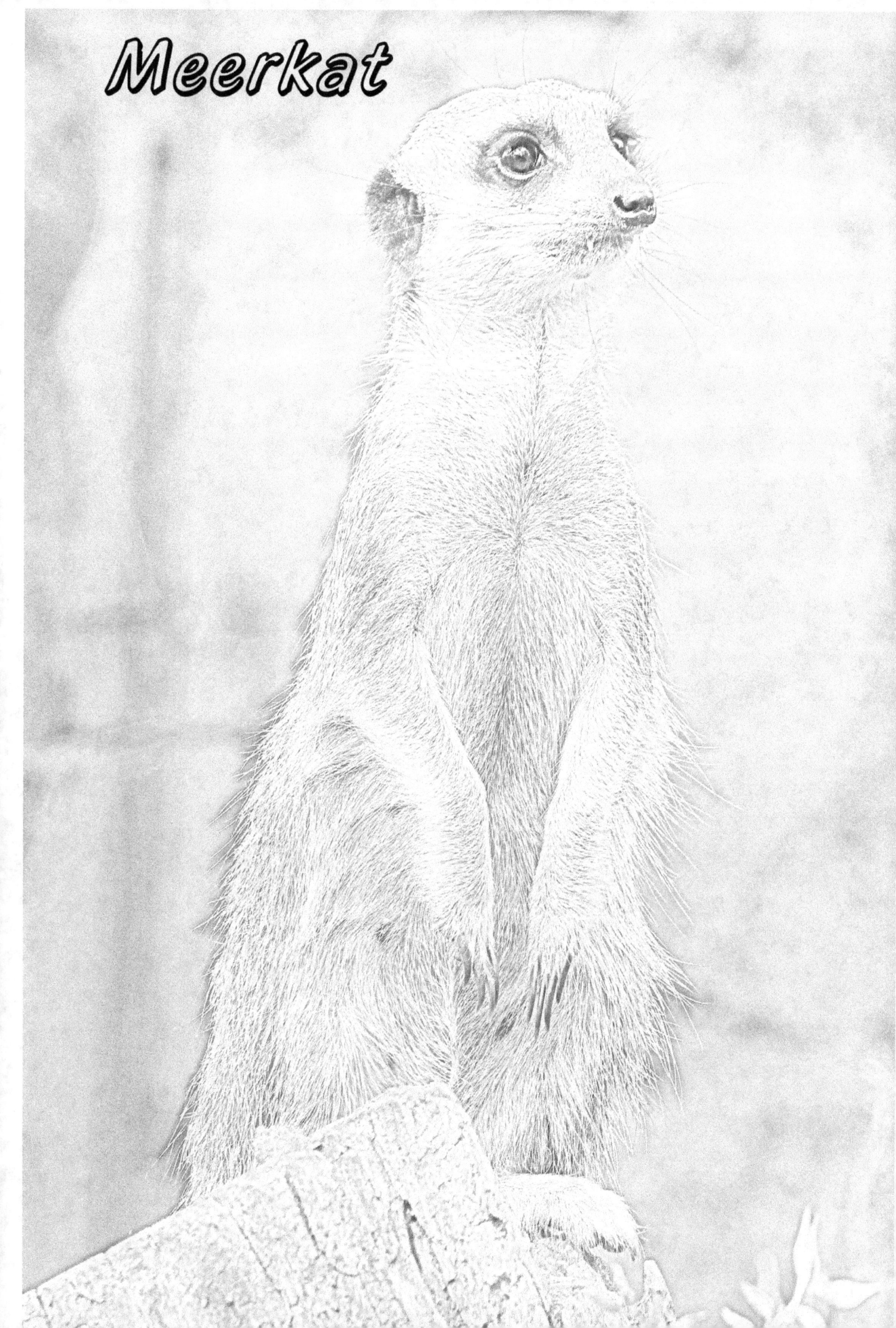

Meerkat

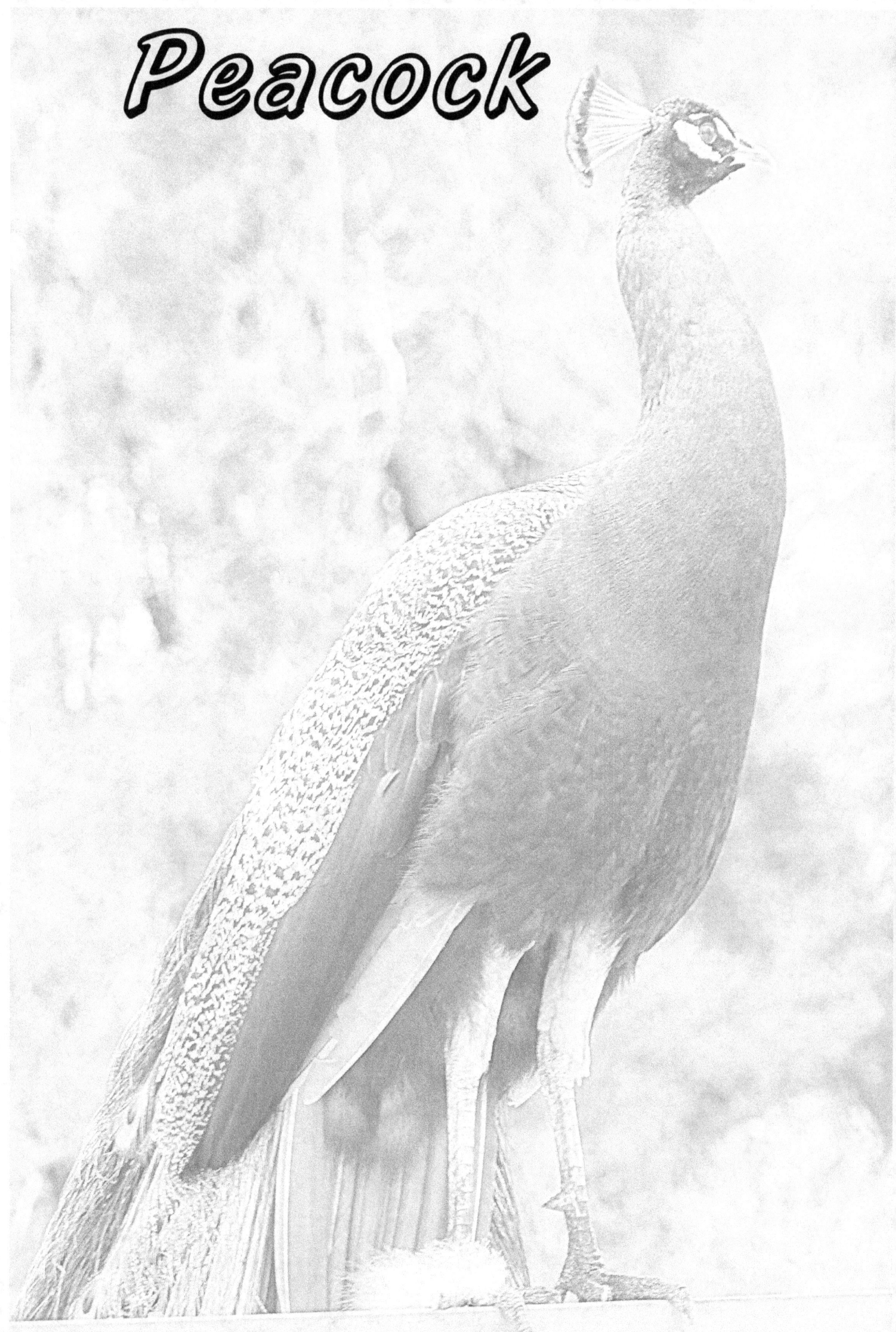

Peacock

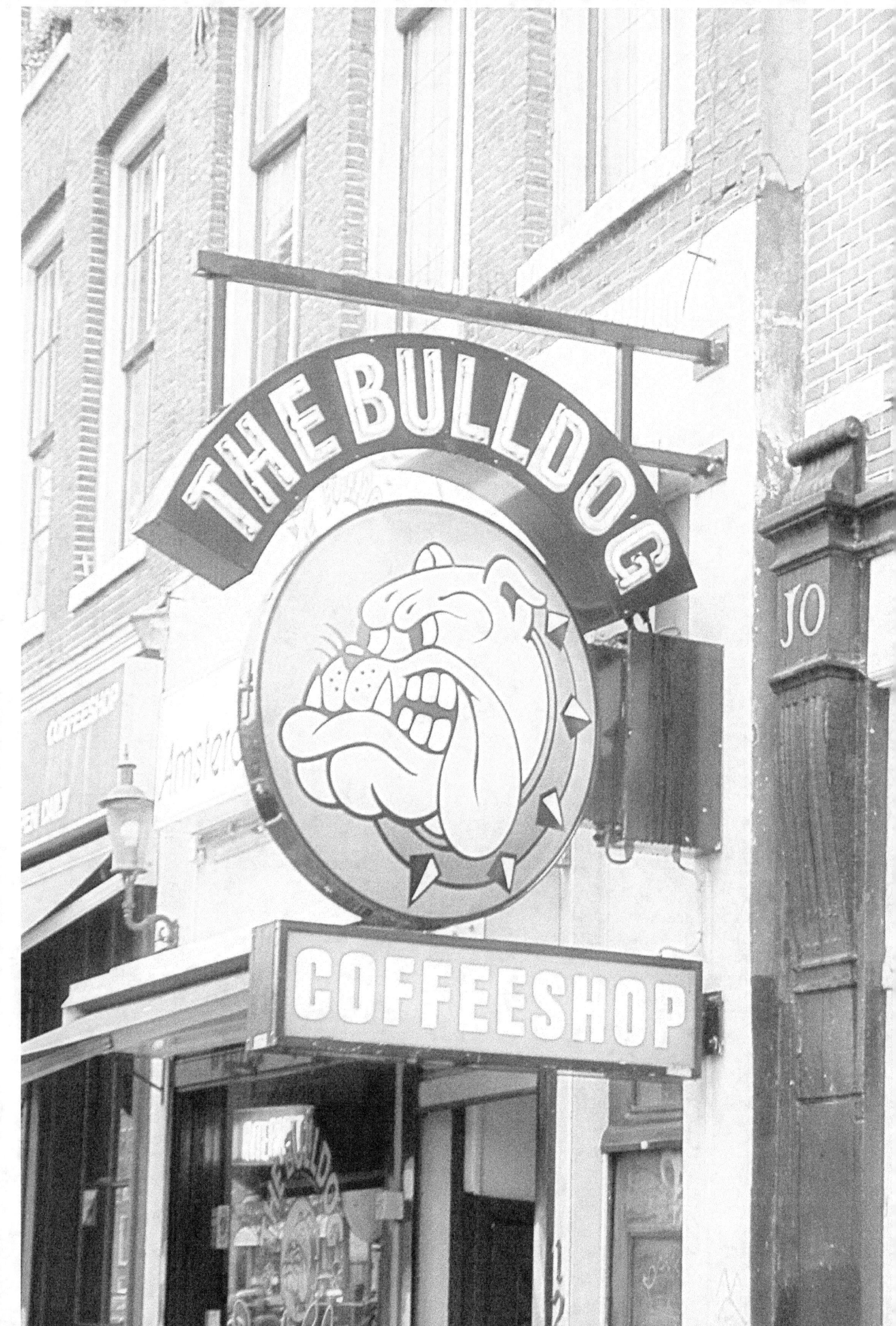

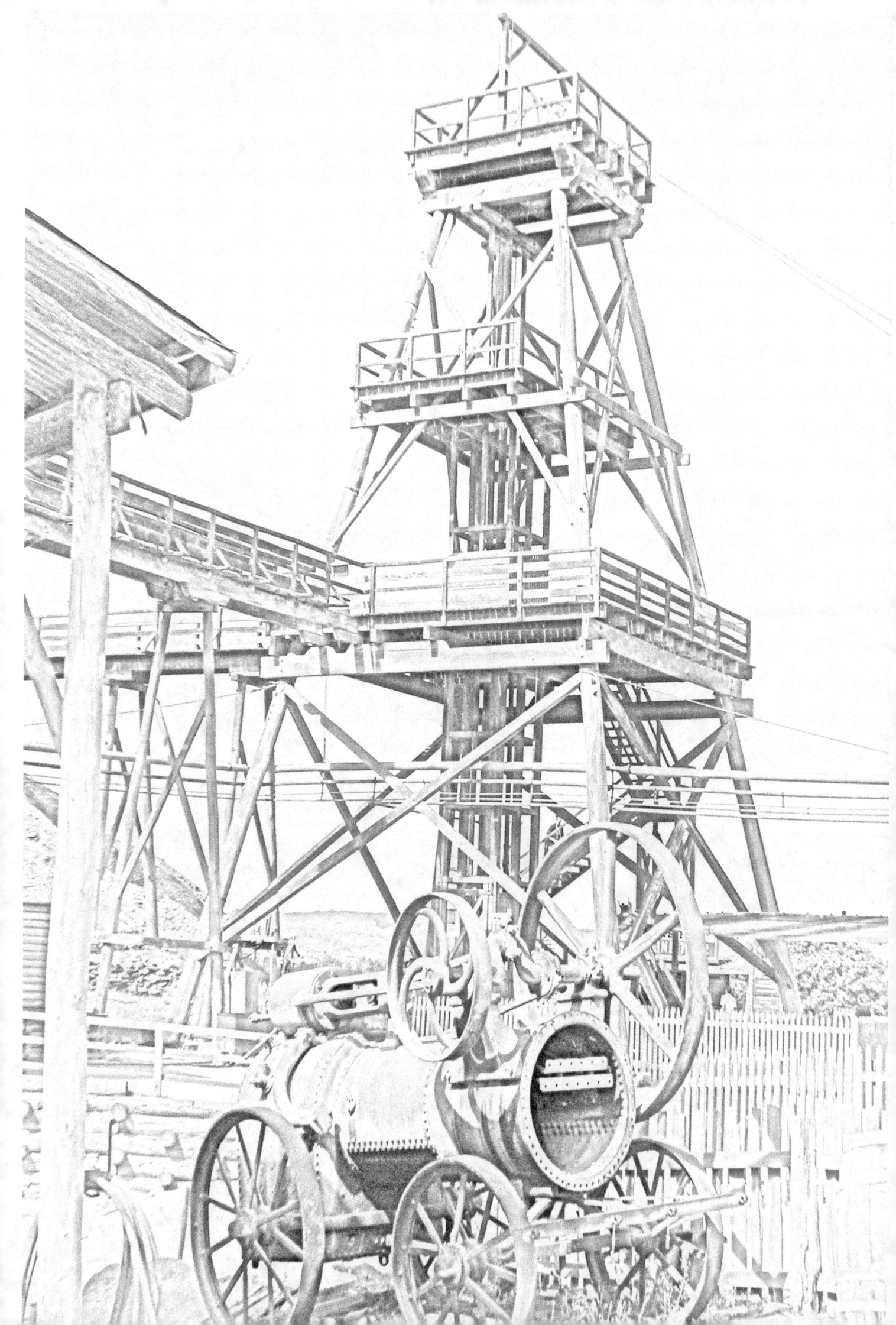

www.ingramcontent.com/pod-product-compliance
Lightning Source LLC
Chambersburg PA
CBHW081049180526
45170CB00005B/1743